The Secret Ship

THE
SECRET
SHIP

*Ruth Klüger
and Peggy Mann*

A true story adapted from *The Last Escape: The Launching of the Largest Secret Rescue Movement of All Time*

DOUBLEDAY & COMPANY
GARDEN CITY, NEW YORK

Library of Congress Cataloging in Publication Data

Aliav, Ruth, 1914–
The secret ship.

SUMMARY: The author relates the tremendous obstacles
involved in the rescue of European Jews who were being
secretly and illegally transported to Palestine on the
ship "Hilda" to escape destruction by the Nazis.
1. Aliav, Ruth, 1914–　　—Juvenile literature.
2. World War, 1939–1945—Jews—Rescue—Juvenile literature. 3. Palestine—Emigration and immigration—Juvenile literature 4. World War, 1939–1945—Personal
narratives, Jewish—Juvenile literature. [1. World War,
1939–1945—Jews—Rescue. 2. Palestine—Emigration and
immigration. 3. Aliav, Ruth, 1914–　　4. World War,
1939–1945—Personal narratives, Jewish] I. Mann, Peggy,
joint author. II. Title.
D810.J4A473　　940.53′1503′924

ISBN 0-385-11328-5
Library of Congress Catalog Card Number 76-2804

This book is adapted from an episode of *The Last
Escape: The Launching of the Largest Secret Rescue
Movement of All Time* by Ruth Klüger and Peggy
Mann, Copyright © 1973 by Ruth Aliav and Peggy
Mann. Published by Doubleday & Company, Inc.

The Secret Ship

1

The Secret Ship *is a true story.*

The background to it is so horrible that today, even those who lived through it say: "It's impossible to believe that it happened."

But it did happen.

It happened just as Adolf Hitler had planned.

Hitler came to power in Germany in 1933. He called himself Der Feuhrer: *The Leader. He said that his Nazi Party would rule in Germany for a thousand years. Sometimes in his screaming speeches he said that his party would rule the entire world for a thousand years.*

Outside of Germany people called him a crackpot. Who was this wild little man with the funny black mustache? Hitler had never finished high school. He had been a tramp in Vienna; he slept in flophouses. His first "steady job" came when he joined the Ger-

man Army. He was never more than a lowly corporal. His officers said he was "too unstable" to be anything more. He also spent seven months in jail.

How could this man have become the leader of Germany?

There were many who asked the question. But most answered it with a shrug. What did it matter how he had risen to the top? He would soon crash to the bottom again.

It happened. But it was not so soon.

On April 30, 1945, Adolf Hitler, deep in a concrete cellar, stuck a pistol into his mouth and blew his brains out.

Nineteen thirty-three to 1945.

Twelve years.

During those twelve years Hitler conquered almost every country in Europe. England, her Commonwealth countries, the United States, and Russia fought back. It was history's most terrible war: World War II.

Millions of people were killed in that war. Millions of soldiers. And millions of civilians—men, women, and children—killed in the bombing raids. And killed by Hitler's armies.

Millions more were killed in another way. They were murdered in huge death camps. Most of these people were Jews.

Hitler had many hates. But those he hated most were Jews. He wanted no Jews in any of the countries he conquered. "If we can't get the Jews out of these countries," Hitler said, "we'll get rid of them—another way."

Most of the death camps Hitler built were in Poland. Jews in all of "Hitler Europe" were rounded up. They were forced into railroad cars which had been built to carry horses and cows. One hundred people were crowded into each cattle car. It was often so crowded they could not even sit on the bare floor. They sometimes had to stand for three or four days and nights. There was no food, little water. Before they reached the death camps, some had already died.

When the trains got to a camp they were met by Nazi soldiers with guns. The Jews were told to get out of the train, and line up.

At some of the camps, like Auschwitz—the largest—10 per cent were "saved" to do slave labor. They were given a bowl of watery soup and a slice of sawdust bread each day.

At most of the death camps no one was saved. They were all sent to "the shower house." If anyone stumbled or tried to hold back he or she was hit with a whip or a club.

Hundreds of people were sent into a shower house

at one time. At Auschwitz there were shower rooms which held two thousand people. Each person had one square foot of space.

When they were packed inside so closely that no one could move, the heavy doors were slammed shut. And locked.

There was no soap in the shower rooms. No water.

Instead, there was gas. Deadly gas.

When all the screaming inside the shower room had stopped, guards—wearing gas masks—opened the heavy metal door. The dead men, women, children were taken out. Their stiff bodies were piled up like stacks of wood. Then, one by one, they were loaded into an oven.

These ovens were unlike any others. They were very long.

They had been specially built to hold human beings.

Before being burned to ashes, however, the body of each murdered man, woman, and child was gone over by a special crew. One worker opened the jaw, knocked out any gold-filled teeth. (In Auschwitz seventeen tons of gold were collected in this way.) Another worker shaved the heads of the women and girls. (The hair was used to stuff mattresses in Germany.) A pile was made of rings, watches, and other such items. They were later sold.

After the bodies were burned, the ashes were used as fertilizer for German fields and flower gardens.

However, the death camps did not start operation until the second year of World War II.

Before the war, and in the early months of the war there was still a chance for Jews to escape. It was difficult—though possible—for them to get out of Germany and the first two countries that Hitler took over: Austria and Czechoslovakia.

There was only one problem.

In all the world there was only one small spot which did not have laws—to keep out Jews. This small spot was Shanghai. But Jews were not welcome, for the city seemed to be sinking with the ever-swelling flood of Jews who fled there.

In all the world there was only one group of people who did welcome the Jews of Europe. These were the Yishuv—the Jews of Palestine.

Part of Palestine later became the nation of Israel.

But from 1920 to 1948 it was the British who ruled in Palestine. During the twelve Hitler years it was the British who ruled in Palestine. And the British set strict limits on the number of Jews who could enter the country.

There were only 817 "Certificates of Entry to Palestine" each month, for all the Jews of Europe—in fact, all the Jews of all the world.

There was, however, another way to get to Palestine. On one of the "secret ships." The British called them "illegal ships." If one of these ships was caught by the British it was taken over. And the "illegals" were sent back to the countries from which they had fled.

The Hilda was one of the secret ships. She was set to sail for Palestine in November 1939—two months after the start of World War II.

A beautiful twenty-five-year-old redhead was in charge of this ship. She was a Palestinian Jew. Her name was Ruth Klüger.

The Secret Ship is the story of the Hilda, a life and death story.

It is also Ruth's story—as she lived it.

6

2

There was a hard knock on the door.

I opened it, and Moshe walked into the room.

"Bad news, Ruth," he said. "Very bad news." His voice seemed to come out of a grave.

From the first time I'd met him it had seemed to me that death clung to him like a cloak. I felt, in fact, that he would die very soon in a horrible way. Yet, to anyone else I suppose that Moshe Orekhovsky looked like—anyone else. He was a short, handsome man with thick black hair, bushy brows and deep-set, light-green eyes. He was thirty-nine years old. When he smiled his face looked younger than his years. But he was not smiling now.

"What bad news?" I said. "What's happened?"

He took a folded yellow paper from the pocket of his overcoat. "They sent this cable to my office, since no one knows where to find you." He handed it to me. "It's from the *Hilda*."

It was a long cable. The words were in Hebrew. We sometimes used this as our code—for few censors knew the ancient language.

> SITUATION HERE DESPERATE. SHIP FROZEN TO PIER. VILLAGERS THREATEN VIOLENCE UNLESS SHIP LEAVES WHEN ICE BREAKS. SAILORS DRUNK, OUT OF CONTROL. WE PLAN TO CABLE OUR STORY TO NEWSPAPERS OF FREE WORLD TO ASK FOR HELP.
>
> SHIP'S COMMITTEE

"My God," I said, when I'd read the words through, "what are we going to do?"

Moshe shrugged. "They leave you, a twenty-five-year-old girl, in charge of an impossible operation. Everything explodes. And you ask *me* what to do. What can I tell you, Ruth?" His hands went out in a helpless gesture.

"Perhaps—the Shamen will help. I'm *sure* he will!" I ran to the telephone.

Shamen was the code name we had given to the one man in Rumania we had found who would help us lease our secret ships. I often thought that "Shamen" was not the most secret code name we could have found for him. Shamen means "fat" in Hebrew. And this man—the Shamen—weighed well over three hundred pounds. He was so fat he had to buy two tickets for himself when he went on an airplane. He could not squeeze into just one seat.

I lifted the telephone receiver, gave the number to the operator. And I listened, frantic, to the steady *brrr brrr brrr* at the other end of the line.

Be there, I prayed silently. *Please. I need you. I don't know what to do.*

I pictured the Shamen heaving his bulk out of the armchair. He would walk slowly to answer the phone. It would take him longer—much, much longer than anyone else to answer. That was why the phone kept ringing. It *must* be why! He *must* be there. He *must* help me!

The *Hilda* was the Shamen's ship. It was he who had hired the seamen. Therefore, he could stop their mutiny. Or, so I hoped and prayed.

But if he stopped the mutiny of the crew, there were still two other "mutinies." Who would help me to handle those?

Moshe took off his coat, hung it on the hook. He took off his gloves, put them in his coat pocket. He started to unwind the long scarf which was like a noose around his neck.

"Wait!" I said suddenly. "Put on your coat. I need you to go to the post office." Quickly, I wrote some words on a scrap of paper. "Please send this cable to the Ship's Committee at once."

"Cable?" he said. "There is no telegraph office in Balchik. No telephone. How can they receive a cable?"

I looked at the address on the cable the Ship's Committee had sent. "Someone somehow got all the way to Bazargic to send this telegram. Perhaps they will wait there for our answer. Please!" I said. "Go. Send this cable."

Moshe looked down at the words I had written. "DO NOTHING YET. TOP PERSON ARRIVING IN BALCHIK TO BRING HELP." He frowned, puzzled. "Who, may I ask, *is* this top person?"

I said, "I am in charge of the ship." My words sounded very faint.

"*You*—a hundred-and-ten-pound girl—are planning to handle a crew of drunken sailors? *You* will—"

"The Shamen will do that." I cut him short.

"The Shamen?" Moshe exploded. "Do you expect that mountain of fat to leave the comforts of Bucharest? Do you expect him to travel over icy roads to that miserable town of Balchik?"

Since I had no answer, I made none. Instead, I said sharply, "Please! The mutiny of the crew is not the most important thing we face right now. The mutiny of the passengers *is!* If they *do* contact the newspapers as they say they will, it will be the end of the ship, the end of everything."

"And the end of *us!*" said Moshe. "We will all land in jail."

"Moshe," I begged, "go to the post office. Send the cable. And I will get ready to go to Balchik."

"*You!*" Again, he spat out the word. But he took his coat from the hook, put on his gloves, rewound his scarf. "Let us hope the line at the post office is a short one. Sometimes it takes two hours of waiting to send a telegram."

"Yes, but the quicker you get there, the faster our cable will reach the ship. Please, Moshe, hurry!"

He left then, closing the door with a slam behind him.

I sat, still, by the telephone, the receiver pressed against my ear. The *brrr brrr brrr* sounded on with the steadiness of a heartbeat. It was senseless, I knew, to sit here waiting. But the telephone was like a life-line to hope.

Hope. Was Moshe right? Would the Shamen turn his back on us? He had every right to.

He, after all, was a Greek shipowner, not a Jew. He often reminded us of this fact. He had some small feeling for what we were trying to do. But most of his concern was for his ships, and the men who sailed them.

We had already stirred his anger with the *Hilda*.

We had told him that his ship would land its secret cargo of human beings in Palestine in early November. It was now December and the *Hilda* had not yet left for Palestine.

Why? Because we were waiting for more fleeing refugees. The Kladovo people, we called them.

We had smuggled them out of Germany and Austria.

Ehud, our man in Austria, had thought up a wonderful plan. He had gone to an Austrian company which ran cruises on the Danube River in the warm-weather months. But no one wanted to take a river cruise when the weather was cold. So the luxury cruise boats stood empty.

Ehud had made a deal with the company. He would lease three river boats in November. They would carry our people down the Danube to the Black Sea. There—so the plan went—they would board the *Hilda*, which would take them to Palestine.

Then the three cruise boats would be returned to their Austrian owner. And all would be done, according to the contract, before the Danube River froze.

All had worked well—up to a point. That point was Kladovo, a Yugoslav village on the Danube River.

The winter of 1939 was one of the coldest in memory. The Danube had frozen earlier than ever before. The three luxury cruise boats reached Kladovo—and could not go on. Ice blocked their way. But they could go back. The western part of the river still was clear of ice.

The fifteen hundred men, women, and children aboard the three cruise boats could not be returned to Austria and Germany. This, we were certain, would mean a return to death.

But the ships *must* be returned. Otherwise our group—the Mossad—would have to pay the full cost of each ship. And this was impossible. We had no money.

So the fifteen hundred men, women, and children were put onto an old oil tanker in the port of Kladovo. Three layers of wooden planks had been quickly built in the belly of the tanker. But there were not enough planks, so the people had to sleep in shifts. Each person was given one thin blanket, which did nothing to hold off the biting cold. They had little to eat: black coffee, noodles, plum jam, and maize bread. That was all.

They were freezing. Starving. And waiting.

Waiting for transit visas.

Kladovo lay on the border of Yugoslavia. To the east was Bulgaria. Across the Danube was Rumania.

We could not go to the Rumanian government to ask for transit visas so that the Kladovo people could cross the country in trains. We could not, because we had been warned that if one more "illegal" ship sailed from any Rumanian port, the ship would be taken by the Rumanians. The people on the ship would be sent back to the countries they came from. And the people who organized the ship would all be thrown into jail.

However, the Bulgarian government was a different matter. The Bulgarians, thus far, had protected their Jews. And what we were asking was, after all, a simple matter. We needed fifteen hundred transit visas, so our people could travel overland to the Bulgarian port of Varna. Our ship, the *Hilda*, would be there—to take them to Palestine.

But the Bulgarian government had, thus far, refused.

They said they had their own Jews to worry about: fifty thousand of them. They could not run the risk of letting fifteen hundred *more* Jews into the country. Even if our people crossed Bulgaria in a sealed train so that no one could get out—even then the "risk" was too great.

Sima Spitzer was the man in charge of the Kladovo people.

He telephoned me almost every night. His voice was shrill. Sometimes he screamed at me over the phone. Every night he said the same thing. "I have a new contact in the government. He says there is a chance for the visas. Yes, a good chance. But only if the ship will be there at the port in Varna to take our people away. The *Hilda* must wait. Without your ship we can never get the visas. *Never!*"

So the *Hilda* was waiting. Waiting in the Rumanian port of Balchik. Balchik was close to the Bulgarian border. As soon as we had the word from Spitzer our ship could leave to pick up his passengers at Varna. That was our plan.

Meanwhile the *Hilda* would wait—in hiding.

It is, of course, no easy matter to hide a ship— even a small twelve-hundred-ton cargo ship like the *Hilda*. But if a ship *can* be hidden, the port of Balchik was the ideal place. This little village was completely cut off in the wintertime. On one side were steep cliffs. On the other side was the Black Sea which, from shore, looked as huge as an ocean. The single road into the village was thick with snow and ice. No car, no bus could travel on it; only a horse and sleigh. Also, the village had no telephone, no cable office. No way to reach the outside world.

For five weeks now the *Hilda* had been waiting in Balchik.

But how long could it continue to wait?

The Fat Man—the Shamen—was already in a fury. He had leased us his ship for one trip to Palestine. When the *Hilda* returned to Rumania, he planned to lease his ship to someone else.

We were cutting into his profits by having the *Hilda* wait in Balchik.

And that was what the Fat Man cared about. His profits!

I sat now staring at the telephone.

The Shamen did not answer.

But there were other people to whom I could turn, for help. For advice.

I put through a call to Schmarya, the American-born member of the Mossad. He was in Greece, trying to find ships. If only he had some possibility of leasing *another* ship for the Kladovo people. Then it would be easier to give the order: let the *Hilda* sail when the ice breaks.

"Please try your call later," the operator said. "All lines to Greece are tied up."

I tried to call Ehud, in Austria.

Kadmon, in Turkey.

Berl Katznelson in Palestine.

The answer was always the same. "Please try your call later. All lines are tied up."

It had been that way since the war broke out. It was almost impossible to get a call through to another country—unless one tried after midnight.

I sometimes had nightmares in which I was being strangled to death by telephone wires. I felt that way now.

Once more I hung up the receiver.

Would I have to make all the decisions alone?

Without the steady *brrr brrr brrr* of the telephone in my ear, the silence in my room swelled suddenly.

It seemed loaded, like a pistol about to go off.

3

One thing was certain.

If I was going to the village of Balchik, there was one supply I must take with me.

Money.

It had been impossible to raise the money we needed *before* the war broke out. Now, it was worse than impossible.

And the only money we had left was in the wall safe downstairs. This was money we had promised to keep for the Shamen. It was in the signed contract. If the *Hilda* was caught, we must have enough money to pay the Shamen for the loss of his ship.

I had no right to touch this money, even though it was I who had raised it.

I had no right. Yet I knew of nothing else that could help me.

I ran downstairs.

My landlord, Mr. Schecter, was in the living room. He sat in his overstuffed armchair, reading the newspaper. He looked up as I came in.

"I'm sorry to trouble you," I said.

"You?" He stood up. "A trouble? When have you ever been a trouble?"

"I'll be leaving Bucharest tonight. Or early tomorrow. I'm taking a trip. I'll need some money. I wonder if you would—open the safe."

"Of course."

I held back the bright-colored woven carpet which hung on the wall, over the safe. Then I looked away, while he turned the dials.

"There." He opened the door of the safe; went back to his armchair. He picked up his newspaper, started to read.

He was a gentleman. He never asked questions. Did he know that he put himself and his wife in danger of arrest by having me live in their house?

He must surely have wondered why I kept two pistols in his wall safe. Yet, he never asked.

I took from the safe four fat envelopes of money: English pounds, Swiss francs, American dollars, Rumanian lei. Then I took out the two pistols and put them, with the envelopes, in my large brown pocketbook.

I closed the safe.

Mr. Schecter looked up. "Do you know when you'll be back?"

"In a few days. At least—I hope so."

He gave me a small smile. "Have a good trip," he said.

Back in my room, I locked the door. And ran to the telephone.

Once again, I tried the Shamen. Again, no answer.

Alexander! Perhaps he would come with me.

I called his number.

As usual, his mother answered. "Yes? Who is it?"

"Is Alexander there?"

"Who wants him?"

"It's Ruth," I said. She knew my voice very well. I called often enough. Yet, she always asked for my name.

"He's not here!" Then she added, "He's never at home any more. He's forgotten he lives here!"

She blamed me, naturally. But in this matter, at least, she was right. Because we kept him so busy, Alexander did stay away from home a good deal.

Of course, she had no idea that her darling son was working with an "illegal" group, called the Mossad. She had no idea that at any moment he might be arrested. She thought he was having an affair with me—and this was what kept him away from home so many nights.

Alexander was my "local."

The Mossad network was spread throughout Europe. But it was a network of only ten members.

Each Mossad member, however, had one or more "locals"; men who knew the country well. Locals were used for small separate jobs. To pick up a set of forged passports. To pay off a man for sending one hundred blankets to our ship.

Most locals knew very little about the Mossad. It was safer that way. But Alexander knew everything.

He was an accountant; careful, well organized. When we gave him a job, we could be certain that it would be done; and well done. That was why I called on him so often. The *only* reason. He was large and clumsy, with fat wet lips and fat fingers. He looked like an overgrown boy.

"Please," I said now to his mother, "it's very important. Ask him to call me as soon as he comes in."

"If I see him," she said crossly. And she hung up the phone.

I lifted the receiver again and gave the operator the number of Arkadi Sloutski.

Arkadi was the Shamen's right-hand man. He was

a Jew—but had long ago forgotten that fact. He helped us only when ordered by the Shamen to do so. And he was only ordered to do so when there was money in the picture for the Shamen.

Again, the phone rang and rang; a mocking sound. I *had* to reach the Shamen—at once. Arkadi was the only person who might know where he was. And I could not reach Arkadi.

There was, however, one thing I could do.

I started to pack. I must go to Balchik—even if I had to make the trip alone.

I put all the sweaters and socks I owned into my old brown suitcase. I had no idea where I would be staying in Balchik. But I was sure it would not be in any well-heated room.

As I closed the door of my wardrobe closet, I stood for a moment, staring at myself in the long mirror on the wardrobe door.

I looked the same as I had the day I left Palestine seven months ago.

How *could* I look the same when I was now—someone else?

I suddenly thought back to that day when it all had started. A warm May morning in Tel Aviv.

Two of the most important men in Palestine had

invited me to lunch. Berl Katznelson was the editor of the Jewish newspaper *Davar*. Eliahu Golumb was the commander-in-chief of the underground Jewish army, the Haganah. I did not know it then, but both men were also founders of the top secret organization, the Mossad: the group set up to smuggle Jews out of Hitler Europe, across the Mediterranean, and through the British blockade into Palestine.

They had questioned me closely, all through lunch.

Then they told me something about the Mossad. And they asked whether I would like to become the tenth member of the group. And the only woman. I would be sent to Rumania, the country in which I had grown up.

"Before you give your answer," Berl warned, "let me tell you this. You will be in danger every day. Our operation is called illegal by every nation in the world. If you're arrested and thrown into prison— we'll have no way to get you out. You may be tortured. You may be killed. We can do nothing to help you."

Eliahu added: "You will be acting as a secret agent. But every other secret agent in the world can return to his homeland and be safe. Not the members of the Mossad. You'll have to go into hiding when you come back home. The British have put a high price on the head of every Mossad member."

"Another thing," said Berl, "you'll have to give up your personal life. You must not tell any friends or relatives where you are going. What you are doing. Secrecy is the keynote of our operation. Secrecy is our only safety."

They paused then, waiting.

"Please," I told them. "I want very much to go. But—why have you chosen *me*?"

"You know nine languages," Berl said. "That's helpful."

"And you look like a teen-aged schoolgirl," Eliahu added. "That's a good cover for a secret agent."

Facing these two men, I *felt* like a teen-aged schoolgirl. I knew nothing. I was nobody. An office worker in Tel Aviv. How could *I* suddenly become a —secret agent? With the most important mission in the world: to save human lives!

I said nothing. But perhaps Berl sensed my thoughts. "You know," he said with a slight smile, "we have not just picked your name out of a hat. You have been—watched, shall I say. Not just you. Many young women. Do you want me to tell you all the reasons that it is you we have chosen as the tenth member of the Mossad?"

They *had* chosen me. I wanted to go. That was enough. Still, there was one question I had to ask. "Will I be thrown into the water? With no one to teach me to swim?"

"You'll not only be given a course in swimming," Eliahu said, "but in lifesaving. You'll work as the assistant of our Mossad man in Rumania. His code name is Kadmon. All the other Mossad men in Europe are in their twenties. Kadmon is almost fifty. Our—elder. Our professor. He'll teach you everything he knows. And he knows a lot."

Three weeks later I'd arrived in Bucharest to meet my new "boss": Kadmon.

He, it turned out, had not been too thrilled at the idea of having me as his assistant. "We're supposed to operate in secrecy," he said sourly. "And they send me a redhead who attracts attention just by walking through a hotel lobby!"

But Kadmon had taught me well. So well that I was now the "Mossad man" in Rumania. And Kadmon had moved on to Turkey where he organized an overland route, smuggling Jews through Syria and into Palestine.

I had organized the *Hilda* alone.

Every day had been a mass of impossibilities. But somehow each problem had been solved.

Now, however, I faced a question no human being should have to solve alone.

Should we wait any longer for the Kladovo people?

Or should the ship sail as soon as the ice broke? If we did, this would mean no visas for the Kladovo people. And that could mean their death warrant.

But how *could* we continue to wait—with three mutinies going on at once? I had to get to Balchik and try to restore some order. And I was certain I could only do that by promising that the ship would leave for Palestine as soon as possible.

There was a knock on the door; our code knock.

I ran to open it.

"Oh, Alexander!" I cried. "Am I glad to see you!"

He was surprised—and delighted—at my greeting.

"Did your mother tell you I called?"

He shook his head. "I haven't been home."

I showed him the cable.

His cheeks were flushed from the cold outside, yet he seemed to go pale. "My God!" he said—the same two words I had spoken when I read the cable.

"Can you come with me to Balchik?"

"Sure," he said, "I'll come with you. But—what can we do? Maybe we can handle our own people.

But the *sailors!* I've seen them when they *weren't* drunk. When they were at work. Even then they were a bad lot, let me tell you."

"I can imagine," I said.

No seaman with his papers in order would sign up to work on a ship which was called "illegal." With good reason. If the ship were caught by the British, the sailor would lose his seaman's papers. Therefore, the only sailors *we* could get were men who had already lost their papers. We called our seamen "pirates." It was a term which fitted well.

"I have some money," I said. "Perhaps the sailors can be bribed to go back to work. In any case, our first step is to go to Balchik. We'll go as far as the Danube by car. After that—" I shrugged. "We'll see."

I asked Alexander to go out and try to rent a car.

And I returned to the telephone.

I am sorry. The lines are all tied up. Would you try your call again.

That was still the answer I got every time I tried to call out of the country.

In between the long-distance calls I tried the Shamen, and his man Arkadi.

Darkness filled the oblong of my window. And snow started to flick on the pane.

Could we start our journey to Balchik in the night? Would the riverboat cross the Danube in the dark? Even this I did not know.

Finally, like a small miracle, the empty *brrr, brrr, brrr* of the telephone was cut short. Someone lifted the receiver at the other end of the line.

"Yes? Hello."

I was so stunned that I forgot for a moment whom I was calling.

"Hello," the voice repeated. "Yes—*hello?*"

It was Arkadi.

"Do you know where the Shamen is?" My words fell out on top of each other. "It's Ruth. I must find him. At once."

"Look," said Arkadi. "How do I know where he is? At some restaurant or nightclub. With some girl. How do I know? Wait till morning."

"I can't wait! Morning will be too late."

"Well, I can't help you."

"DON'T!" I shouted. "Don't hang up. Please!" Somehow then I talked him into making the rounds of restaurants and nightclubs to look for the Shamen.

It was two in the morning when the Shamen finally telephoned. He was angry. "Well, what is it? Why do you bother me in the nighttime?"

"Your crew is on the point of mutiny," I told him. "They are drunk. Out of control."

"Well," said the Shamen, "who can blame them? Sitting in that Godforsaken place for weeks! I'll tell you what you can do."

"Yes! Please! What?" This was what I needed. Advice.

"Take your people off the *Hilda*. Give me back my ship. I'll lease it to someone else. Someone *legal*. The sailors will be fine as soon as they know they're on a regular ship. Doing a regular job. You've already broken your contract. You've kept the ship in Balchik for five weeks waiting for—God knows what. I leased you a ship. Not a sitting hotel. I want my ship back!"

"Oh, please—" There were tears behind my words. I pretended I had not heard what he said. "I'm leaving for Balchik at dawn. Please come with me. Please help me. You are the only one I can turn to. The only one I can count on."

His answer was a curse.

He hung up the phone.

4

Alexander and I planned to leave Bucharest at dawn.

He had managed to rent a car, and I sent him home to get some sleep. I, too, tried to sleep; not knowing when I would sleep again. Or where.

But there were too many problems. There was too much fear. Over and over I prayed that the telephone would ring. I had placed six overseas calls. If only one of them would come through. From Kadmon. From Ehud. From someone who could tell me what to do.

Suddenly, the jarring sound of the phone split the stillness of my room.

I jumped out of bed, ran to answer.

"Yes? Hello."

"Spitzer here."

Sima Spitzer! The one person I did not want to

hear from. The one person who seemed always able to get through.

Spitzer was not a Mossad member. He was head of the Jewish community in Belgrade. He had taken on the project of getting the Bulgarian transit visas for the Kladovo people. Again and again he had gone to government officials. He was told to try here—and there. He met with this official—and that. He received many promises. They all fell through.

But there still was hope. After all, he asked for so little. *Transit* visas, that was all! So that fifteen hundred human beings—including two hundred and fifty children—could cross Bulgaria locked in a sealed train.

There was hope, yes. But *only* if the Bulgarian officials were certain that a ship—our ship—would be waiting to take the Jews away.

Tonight when he phoned I said, "Spitzer, I have good news for you. Our ship cannot leave for Palestine yet. It is frozen to the pier."

"*Frozen?*"

"Yes," I said. "Can you imagine!"

"An act of God!" Spitzer exclaimed. "The Black Sea is salt water. But it is so cold that even salt water freezes! It is a sign, I tell you. Maybe God looked down and saw our people—how they are living in Kladovo. Their feet are swollen with frostbite. They are starving. God has seen the hell on board that ship. He has sent a sign. He will help us."

"Let us hope so," I said.

After the call I lay awake staring up into the darkness.

I had never in my life felt more alone.

I was twenty-five years old. In another life, a normal life, I might be out with a man I loved at the theater, or dancing, or walking through the woods at the edge of the city.

And there *was* a man I loved. Stefan. Stefan Meta. I had loved him since I was a young girl growing up in the Rumanian town of Czernowitz. Stefan was a friend of my older brother, David. How often as a schoolgirl had I written his name in the margin of my notebooks. *Stefan Meta.* Sometimes I wrote *Madame Stefan Meta* (me). He, of course, had seen me only as David's little sister.

I was sixteen when I left Czernowitz to go to the University of Vienna. I was nineteen when I left for Palestine.

But—I was twenty-five when I went back to Czernowitz—the week after World War II broke out. And Stefan no longer saw me as David's little sister.

I'd returned to Czernowitz for two reasons. To try

to raise money so that we could lease the *Hilda* from the Shamen. And to try to persuade my brother David to take his family to Palestine.

I had also gone hoping that I would see Stefan again.

We did not have much time together.

But there was time enough to fall in love.

When I left Czernowitz Stefan brought me to the station. We kissed good-by, clinging together.

On the train I made my way through the crowded corridor to an open window. I searched for him in the crowd. *Stefan, where are you?*

I needed to see him one more time. I might never see him again. *Stefan, my love, where are you?*

As the train started to move, soot, and cinders swept in through the open window, along with a cooling breeze. Then the lights of the city fell away in the distance. The train sped on, between the darkness of fields and sky.

I found that I was weeping.

You'll have no time for a personal life. Berl had warned me before I agreed to join the Mossad. It was true. There was no time.

I had raised the money we needed to lease the *Hilda*.

I would be busy now night and day until the ship sailed.

As I stood there in the crowded train corridor crying, I felt a heavy hand on my shoulder.

I turned.

Stefan was beside me. He moved so that he could hold me. I raised my face and we kissed.

People were pressing tight around us. Yet, we were alone.

He said something. But his words were blotted out by the noise in the corridor and the sound of the train wheels.

"What?" I said.

He lifted me off my feet, held me so that his lips were close to my ear. "I want to marry you," he said. "Will you marry me?"

"Yes," I said.

He set me back on my feet. But his arms were around me, holding me hard against him.

"Will you come to Palestine?" I said.

"If I must."

"You must."

He nodded. "I'll try to sell my house, my business. As soon as I do, I will come to you."

I could not tell him—not even Stefan my love—that if I did return to Palestine, I would have to go into hiding. He knew nothing of my work with the Mossad.

He saw me only as David's little sister—who had

suddenly grown up. David's sister, with whom he had suddenly fallen in love.

The train had slowed then. The lights of a station glowed through the darkness.

Stefan took a gold ring from his finger, pressed it into my hand. "Keep this. Our engagement ring."

We clung, kissing.

The train drew to a stop.

"I'll get off here," Stefan said. "I'll phone you at the apartment tomorrow night."

He made his way through the corridor, to the door. And I leaned out the window waving to him until the train started to move, pulling us apart.

5

Stefan's ring was too large for my finger. I wore it on a chain around my neck.

Now, as I lay in bed, I held his ring hard in my hand. The ring brought him closer. He had taken this ring from his finger to give to me.

Stefan . . . will we ever be able to live out our love?

He had wanted to come to Bucharest to be with me. But I had no time. He could not understand. How could I say that I loved him but that I had no time?

Of course he could not understand. Nor could I explain. I told him that I was on a mission—to sell land, orange groves, in Palestine. This, in fact, was my "cover"; for the police, for anyone who asked what I was doing in Rumania. It was a good cover. It gave me reason to approach rich Jews for money. But

Stefan could not understand why *this* job kept me busy night and day.

"When you come to Palestine," I kept telling him, "we'll be together then."

But was he really trying to sell his home, his business? Did he really intend to leave Rumania? Or was he like the others whom I had begged to leave—now, while there still was time?

Look, they all told me, *relax! It won't happen here. Not in Rumania!*

How many times had I heard that? *It can't happen here.* The sentence shattered my dreams. That simple sentence which was, I felt certain, a death sentence.

My sister-in-law Sophie had screamed at me when I told David he should take his family and get out. Now. Today. While there still was time.

"*Leave?*" Sophie had shouted. "You must be crazy! We've just bought this apartment . . . ordered new furniture . . . had the whole place repainted. And you tell us to *leave?* You're insane!"

I had pointed out to Sophie—and to my brother David—that the Germans were, right at that moment, raging through Poland. And this fine, newly repainted apartment was not very far from the Polish border.

"No, Ruth!" Sophie cried. "Only cowards run!

What would happen to the world if everyone, at the first sign of danger, packed up and started running somewhere else? You *stay!* That's how you help the world keep its balance. You stay in the place where your children go to school . . . where their friends are . . . where *your* friends are. . . . You stay on the block where your house is. You stay where you know the shopkeepers . . . where your doctor is . . . your dentist is . . . your beauty parlor is. You *stay!*" She screamed the words at me. "*You stay!*"

So they had stayed.

And now Poland had fallen to the Germans. Poland with its three and a half million Jews.

Would Rumania be next on Hitler's list?

I did not sleep again that night.

Usually I closed the shutters when I slept. But this time I had left them open. It was as though I might find some answers by staring up at the sky.

The first cold fingers of dawn stretched through the darkness. I lay in bed, watching the night fade.

There was a soft knock on the door. But it was not our code knock. It could not be Alexander. He knew the code. Who else would be coming here at dawn? The police?

I got up, pulled on my robe, went to the door.

"Who is it?"

"Arkadi."

Relief washed through me. "A moment." I unbolted the door, pulled the light cord.

A furry figure entered the room. If he had not said his name I would never have known him. Arkadi, usually so well dressed in dark suit and high-shined shoes, was now merely a face inside a huge fur jacket and fur hat. His boots were far too big for his small feet. He seemed to be dressed for an Arctic trip.

"The Shamen told me to come with you," he said, as he took off his jacket. He had three sweaters underneath.

"Are you dressed warmly enough?" I asked him.

Arkadi smiled. "Don't worry. Sitting next to you I'll be warm enough."

He was rather put out when I told him that Alexander would be coming with us.

We left Bucharest an hour later in a car which rattled nosily down the empty city streets.

When the war started, everything became hard to get. And "everything" included cars for hire. This ancient automobile was the only one Alexander had been able to find. It sounded as though it would fall to pieces on the road. I prayed it would take us as far as the Danube River.

Alexander drove.

Arkadi and I sat in the back seat. He was in the best of moods and told me tales of his life as a ship's captain in Russia and Greece.

When he asked why I was so gloomy, I said, "I'm tired, that's all." I was afraid if I told him all the troubles in Balchik, he would insist we drive him right back home again.

Better to wait till we neared Balchik before we told him too much. He knew only that he was being sent to get the sailors back onto the ship. And this, he thought, would not be too hard a job—since we had money to bribe them with.

It was noon by the time our old car made it down to the Danube and the river ferry. The boatman told us there was no need to pay a crossing fee for our car. "You'll have no use for a car on the other side of the river," he said. "The roads are thick with snow and ice. You'll have to rent a horse and sleigh if you want to go on."

And it turned out that he had a brother-in-law who would be happy to rent us a horse and sleigh.

"Can he take us all the way to Balchik?" I asked.

The boatman laughed. "Balchik, young lady, is a long way from here. Especially in the wintertime. But my brother-in-law will take you to the home of my cousin. There you'll change horses and sleigh. Our cousin will take you on another twenty miles. To the home of his uncle. We have it well worked out. You'll reach Balchik. But," he added, "you may be frozen solid by the time you get there."

I felt more gloomy and scared than ever as we sat on the ferry. The boat had walls and a roof. But this did little to keep out the cold. The winter wind rushed down the river and knifed into every crack in the walls. I tried to sink down into my landlady's old fur coat. Mrs. Schecter had insisted I borrow it when she heard I was taking a trip into the countryside.

I was the only woman aboard. The other passengers, all peasants, sat on a bench across from us and stared at me. Some smoked on strong, stinking pipes. Others chewed on raw onions and black bread. Some carried live chickens and geese with feet tied together. The squawking of the birds blended strangely with the whistling wind.

When we finally reached the other side, the boatman went off to find his brother-in-law. We waited on the boat.

Arkadi, who had started the trip like a tourist on a holiday, was now sour and glum. "The Shamen should have come himself," he said, shivering. "At least he has his fat to keep him warm."

"Pity the poor horses," I said, "if they had to pull *his* weight in the sleigh!"

Arkadi did not even trouble to smile.

The boatman's brother-in-law looked like a hill of rags. Scarves were wound around his head, face, neck. Only his eyes showed. His two horses were also well covered with blankets. Their breath hung on in the frosty air.

I sat between Arkadi and Alexander. The driver buried our feet and legs in straw. Then he put horse blankets over us. And he wrapped heavy rags around our faces. The rags smelled of onions and sweat.

All this padding helped but little when we left the town and came onto the open road. Freezing winds swept across the fields. I had never been so cold.

In the car and on the ferry when I'd thought of the problems waiting for us in Balchik, fear rose within me. Now it seemed that even the fear froze. I could think only of one thing. When would we reach the uncle's house so that we could sit in front of a fire and thaw out?

But when we finally did stop at the home of the cousin's uncle, it was only to change horses and sleigh. We had a cup of hot tea, black bread, dried ham. Then we moved on. We had to, the uncle said. Otherwise, we would never reach Balchik by nightfall. And we would certainly freeze to death if we had to spend a night on the road.

We drove on past snow-blanketed fields. Sometimes we passed a few mud-brick huts, half hidden by snow. We drove over streams and small rivers, each frozen solid as a road. The sun glinted sharp on the white stretches of ice and snow. But even the sunlight seemed frozen.

Finally, we reached the home of the uncle's nephew, who ran a pub. This time we did have time to thaw out. The nephew said he would not take us on to Balchik. It was too late in the day, and too cold.

While Arkadi and I sat gratefully before the fire, Alexander argued with the nephew.

"All right," the young man said at last. "I'll take you. But I must have twice the price you paid my uncle."

Alexander agreed.

At which point the uncle spoke up. "Why should

I not have the same double money as my nephew? I took you just as far as he will!"

Again, Alexander could do nothing but agree.

Whereupon Arkadi stood up and said that we would all stay the night at the pub. He looked at me. "They have two free rooms here. I asked already. So we will have a good dinner, a good sleep. And we'll go on in the morning."

I shook my head. "We *must* get there tonight."

"But why?" he exploded. "Let the sailors have one more night of drinking. What's the difference? What's the big rush?"

"Sit down," I said. "It's time to tell you *all* the bad news about the *Hilda*."

He sat down. He listened quietly. Then he stared at me. "What are you talking about?" he said. "I will commit suicide."

He started yelling at me. He grew so excited that specks of spit shot out of his mouth.

"Why didn't you tell me these things?" he shouted. "I would never have come!"

"That's why I didn't tell you. We need you. Only you can handle the sailors on that ship. You or the Shamen." Then, before his anger erupted again, I said quickly, "Arkadi, remember the first time we met? At the home of the Shamen. I came there with

45

Kadmon. And when you had heard what we had to say, you thanked us. You thanked us for making you remember that you were a Jew. A Jew who—could help."

"Sure," said Arkadi. "It's easy enough to make fine speeches when you're sitting in a comfortable room on a warm spring day in Bucharest."

At least he remembered the scene.

"Well"—I stood up—"Alexander and I *must* get to Balchik by nightfall. If our passengers start sending those cables, we are lost. They, and we, and all the others we still may be able to save."

Arkadi shrugged. "That may be. But the fact is, there is still no rush about *me* getting to Balchik. It will take me at least twelve hours to thaw out. I'll stay here tonight and I'll come along to Balchik tomorrow."

A half hour later the cousin announced that his horses and sleigh were ready. I stood up. Arkadi did too. I thought he was going upstairs to his room.

But he was the first to take his seat in the sleigh.

6

We had been well warned. We *must* reach Balchik before nightfall.

But we did not.

The final miles were filled with terror. The two horses trotted slowly over the ice-glazed road, with only the frosty moonlight to show the way.

I remembered all the tales I'd heard about this district. A land of smugglers, cutthroats, and thieves. My only comfort was the thought that no one in his right mind would venture out for anything on a night as bitter cold as this. Yet, I still kept "seeing" them there in the darkness, waiting to jump out and murder us all.

Finally, the village of Balchik came into view. We were welcomed by a snarling, yapping pack of dogs who followed our sleigh down to the pier.

The *Hilda* loomed like a black monster. Moonlight cast a faint chilled brightness on the ice which held the ship prisoner. We could see a few dark shapes moving on deck. They aimed their flashlight beams in our direction.

Sharp wind cut in from the open sea. It seemed to shove us into our seats. No one spoke. No one moved.

At last, Arkadi said, "Well, I may as well have a look for the captain." He climbed down from the sleigh, screamed. Then he fell to his knees.

"What's wrong?" I cried.

"Nothing at all!" he answered. "But wait till *you* try walking on frozen legs!" With a stream of Russian curses he crawled through the ice-crusted snow till he reached the gangplank. Several of the dark shapes on deck came down to help him aboard.

Alexander told the driver how to reach the mayor's house. I would wait there while Alexander boarded the *Hilda* and found members of the Ship's Committee. Then he would bring them to see me.

When he got out of the sleigh, Alexander, too, fell to his knees. Like Arkadi, he started crawling, cursing his way through the snow to the ship.

Then the driver snapped his reins, and we took off.

The mayor's house was on top of a small hill.

When we reached it, the driver turned and said to

me, "Well, you are lucky. At times I thought we would never make it. It is not safe, as you know, to drive these roads in the nighttime. Of course, if one of my horses had broken his leg, you'd pay for a new horse. As it is, I will only charge you double the price we agreed on."

I felt unable to argue. Indeed, I felt unable to move. "Please help me inside," I said. "Then you will be paid."

He lifted me out of the sleigh, carried me in his arms. Then he kicked at the front door.

It was opened by a fat man with a very red nose.

"What's wrong with her? Is she dead?" he asked.

The driver walked into the room. He put me down in a chair by the fireplace.

I took the rags from around my face. "I would like to see the mayor," I said.

"I am the mayor," said the fat man. "Who are you?"

I told him that I had come from Bucharest to take charge of the ship.

The mayor gave a shout of laughter. "They say they are sending a top man from Bucharest to take charge of the ship. A man who will solve all our problems. And what do they send. *You!*"

"Look here," said the driver, stamping the snow from his boots, "we're half frozen. Can you let us have something hot to drink?"

The mayor opened his mouth wide and yelled, "Anna!"

A fat woman in a heavy nightgown came in from the next room.

"Madame," I said, "I hope you will forgive us. We did not mean to bother you in the middle of the night."

She stared at me and said nothing at all.

I turned to the mayor. "I am told it is not safe for a woman to stay the night at the pub. I have come to ask you for help. Where in Balchik can I rent a room?"

"Here, of course," said the mayor. "There is no other place. We have a guest cabin out back. The price," he added, "is a thousand lei a night." It was more than the cost of a room in the finest hotel in Bucharest. But again, I did not have the strength to bargain. I nodded.

The mayor raised his voice to a lordly shout, though his wife stood but a few feet away. "Anna! Go get the guest room ready."

As she turned to leave, he shouted again. "Wait. First get our visitors something hot to eat and drink."

As we sipped the steaming hot soup, the mayor sounded off about our ship.

"This is a peaceful village! Suddenly seven hundred strangers are upon us. Your sailors are drunk in the streets. They fight with each other. And with our men. They put fear into our women and children. And your cursed ship! There—like a house of evil in our peaceful bay. The noise! And the smell! I was on that ship for ten minutes! It was all I could take of the stink! They throw their droppings—their garbage —into our fine blue bay. And now that the water is frozen, it all goes onto the ice! It is a wonder sickness has not swept through our town. As mayor of Balchik I must demand that your ship leaves our port. You can buy my silence no longer. If your ship does *not* leave, I will cable the police in Bucharest. They will get rid of your stinking ship soon enough!"

I said I was sorry for the trouble our ship had brought. "But," I pointed out, "perhaps some good came with the bad. We have, after all, paid well for the food and other things we bought in your town."

"*What?*" he shouted. "You say that is *good?* Your people have bought up everything in our stores. Our shelves are empty. Now we must go all the way to Bazargic for the things we need. You have seen yourself what it is like to travel these roads in the winter!"

I had seen, indeed. I changed the subject quickly. I told the mayor that I had not slept for thirty-six hours. And I asked whether I might go to my room.

7

The guest cabin was a storage shed. It had no window. It had no heat. It was many yards from the main house. There was a straw-filled mattress on the floor. This was covered with a dirty quilt and a horse blanket. There was a small bench which held a kerosene lamp—the only light. Burlap bags and crates were piled against the wall.

"The outhouse is in the back," the mayor said. "And here is your private towel." He gave it to me with some pride. Then he turned to leave. "Sleep well. The door," he added, "has no lock. But don't worry. No one will trouble you. Not here in the house of the mayor of Balchik."

The door not only had no lock, it did not even close properly. It would be like sleeping in the bitter cold open air.

I wound a scarf around my face and crawled under

the quilt and horse blanket. I had on all the clothes I'd brought with me, including boots and my landlady's fur coat.

Life had begun to come back to my frozen fingers and toes and they ached painfully. I suddenly remembered Sima Spitzer's frantic words. "They are freezing to death," he had shouted at me on the telephone. "Each has one thin blanket. Their feet are swollen with frostbite."

Fifteen hundred men, women, children trapped on a boat in the Danube. Trapped and waiting.

Tomorrow would I have to decide the fate of fifteen hundred men, women, and children? Two hundred fifty children? Their faces seemed to peer at me from the darkness.

What had they done, these fifteen hundred human beings—why had they been forced to flee from their homes? Why did they have to leave the lives they had built as carefully as anyone's? Why must they suddenly have to look for a new land— some place in this world—where they could live? What had they done that there was no country to stretch out a hand of help, or welcome?

Why were they not even given the right to cross Bulgaria in a sealed train? On their way to— someplace else.

Why?

Because they were Jews.

Was *that* an answer?

WHY? The question rang out louder—louder. But there was no answer. Only the question. WHY?

It was a question which no one answered. It was a question which no one even heard!

After a while I fell into a deep black cave of sleep.

I dreamed of Stefan.

He entered my dreams almost every night. They were often dreams of the life we would have when the world was at peace and we were married. Simple dreams which seemed, when I woke, like miracles of impossible wonder.

On this night I dreamed that Stefan was sitting in the sunlight on the terrace of our Tel Aviv apartment. He was reading the newspaper. In Hebrew. I was in the kitchen, making breakfast. I squeezed two tall glasses of fresh orange juice. Then I made him scrambled eggs. "Darling," I called out to him, "how do you like your eggs? Soft or—" I looked up, pressed my hands over my mouth. I did not even know how Stefan liked his scrambled eggs. I had never had time to find out. I went to the balcony to ask him. But his chair was empty. He had gone. Had he even been there?

I woke up crying.

Then I lay looking at the door of the shed. It had

no lock and did not even close all the way. I imagined booted bearded men shoving open the door, pulling me up from my straw mattress, ripping off my clothes to find the envelopes of money hidden in my brassiere.

I was, in fact, awakened early the next morning by booted, bearded men.

Alexander knocked at the door of the shed. Then he came in. A group of men stood outside, backed by the thin, gray light of early morning.

"My God," Alexander exploded, "this place is like sleeping on an iceberg. Are you all right?" Without waiting for my answer, he told me that the Ship's Committee was outside. "They wanted to meet with you last night. I was able to keep them off until this morning. But now you must see them."

I got out of bed. My nose felt like an ice cube, my fingers like ten stiff icicles. But otherwise, I was warm. The layers of clothing had kept in my body heat. And I had slept as though I were drugged.

I thanked Alexander for holding off the meeting until this morning. I now felt better able to deal with problems.

Alexander opened the door wide, and they came in.

"Dr. Sand," said Alexander. "Dr. Adler. Dr. Grubler. Dr. Zentner." Each man nodded at me, and then stared, or glared.

There were thirteen of them. Five doctors. Two lawyers. A restaurant owner, Arthur Loewy. A textile salesman, Hans Klein; and several others.

The doctors stood in a line against the wall. The others sat on boxes, crates, and on the bed. Alexander and I stood facing them, as though they were the enemy.

That is what they sounded like. They all burst out at once with loud complaints.

"Please!" My word was sharp as a shot.

It was followed by dead silence.

"We'll get nothing done," I said, "if you all speak at once."

"All right," said Willi Thein, one of the lawyers. "I'll let you have it in one sentence. We can no longer control our people. We've had to let them off the ship to get at the snow. The snow has kept us alive, since we've run out of water. Each night we try to count how many are aboard. But we can't. The ship's too crowded. There's no more order. For all we know, some may have taken off already. Tried to make their own way to Bucharest. They want to tell the world what's going on here."

Alexander cursed.

Willi Thein looked at him. "Oh yes, it's fine for you, my friend! You come here. You give out a few orders. Then you take off. Go back to Bucharest. Back to your apartment. Tell me, do you have heat in your place? Hot and cold running water? It's been weeks since any of us had a bath. You sleep in a bed with a mattress and sheets. Not on a board with two feet of space between it and the board above you—where someone else sleeps. Or tries to."

I broke in. "Let's hear all your problems. One by one. We'll try to find some way to help."

"*You!*" said Hans Klein. "You are the first problem! We told our people a top man from the organization is coming here. When they see a *woman*—! Not even a woman. A *girl!*"

"They won't see her," Alexander said. "None of the Mossad people are ever seen by the passengers. It's a rule."

Klein nodded. "Well, that's good. But the real question is, how can *she* solve our problems?"

They spoke to each other over my head, as though I were not even there.

"Look," I said, "just tell me your problems. One by one. We'll try our best to help."

Each member of the Ship's Committee had a different problem which he regarded as *the* most important.

The restaurant owner said they were all on the point of starving. There was nothing left to eat on the ship except frozen bread. And cans of spaghetti and beans.

I told him that I had brought money with me. We would take horses and sleighs to the town of Bazargic. "We'll buy out the town!" I said.

A few of the men smiled, others nodded. The stiffness in the room seemed to soften.

"Very good," said Dr. Zentner. "And the first two people to get on those sleighs must be the two pregnant women we have on board."

It was the first I had heard of this. "How—pregnant are they?"

"They may give birth any minute."

"I thought," said Willi Thein, turning on me, "you did not allow pregnant women on Mossad ships."

"We don't," I told him. "Not if we know. No pregnant women. And no sick people. The trip is hard enough for those who are in the best of health."

"Well," said Dr. Zentner, "there is a hospital in Bazargic. So we'll get rid of *that* problem. One, two, three—easy."

I knew it would not be so one-two-three easy. I knew we could not take the two women to the hospital in Bazargic. The risk was too great. Bazargic was a town with telephones and a cable office. The news of the two pregnant women from a "secret ship" might start a spark of interest. The spark could flare into a flame—which would mean the end of the ship. The end of all of us.

I turned to the doctors. "It seems we have plenty of doctors on board our ship. And there is a private place. The captain's cabin. We can turn that into a hospital room."

"The captain," said Dr. Zentner, "has other uses for his cabin."

"Perhaps," I said, "we can talk to him—with money."

Dr. Zentner shrugged. "We have enough troubles on board. No one wants two screaming babies on the trip to Palestine."

Then they brought up the subject of the Turkish bath.

It stood on top of a hill behind the village. It had not been used for eighty years. The Ship's Committee now wanted me to get the bath working again. It seemed that each of the Hilda's passengers had the same dream. To have a bath.

"It's more than just getting clean," said Dr. Sand. "It's more than getting rid of lice. To have a hot bath would mean, somehow, to have new hope."

I understood this. How many times, dead with

tiredness, worn with despair, had I lain in a hot bath. I knew how helpful it could be. I also knew the other members of the Mossad would think me mad if I paid money to have the Turkish bath put back in working order. We needed the little money we had for life-and-death matters. The people on board the *Hilda* were lucky enough to be there. It might be the last of our secret ships to sail from Europe. What did it matter whether or not our passengers had a hot bath?

But it did matter. Deeply. I knew this.

"I'll—speak to the mayor," I said finally. "I promise you—if possible, everyone on the ship will have a bath."

"What about the crew?" said Loewy. "How will you get them back to the ship?"

Then every man on the Ship's Committee jumped in with his own horror tales about the crew. The drunkenness. The knife fights. The fear they brought to the women passengers, and to the women and young girls of Balchik.

"A fine lot of sailors you've found for us!" Hans Klein exploded. "One of them told me last night he could never go home to Greece. He was wanted for murder!"

"And why a crew of Greeks and Turks?" asked Willi Thein. "Even when things are at their best,

Greeks and Turks always seem to be at each other. But here—stuck in the ice—with nothing to do, nowhere to go—"

"Look!" I cut in sharply. "It is no easy job to get any sailor to sign onto an illegal ship. If such a ship is caught by the British, every sailor on it loses his seaman's papers. The captain risks three years in prison. So who can we get as sailors? Only men who have already lost their seaman's papers. Only men who have nothing more to lose."

They were silent. I went on, "We have our weapon for dealing with the crew. Money. Arkadi will give a bonus of one hundred pounds sterling to every crew member who returns to the ship and does his job well. He'll get fifty pounds when the ship sails. The other fifty when the *Hilda* returns to a European port."

"Money may help bring some of them back to the ship," said Willi Thein. "But what about the others —the thieves, the drunks, the murderers? We'll need something better than money to bring *them* back into line."

I undid my fur coat, took off the holster. "Would a pair of pistols help you?"

"Yes!" said Thein. He held out his hand for the pistols.

"You know something about guns." I said it as a statement. But it was also a question.

"I was an officer in the Czech Army," said Willi Thein.

I gave him the pistols.

"Perhaps," said Hans Klein, "you've also brought a few secret weapons for use with some of the passengers. There are some who will need more than a hot bath. Or a good meal. One girl already tried to kill herself. Many are talking of going back home. The Czechs, especially. No hell, they say, could be worse than the one they're living in now—on your ship. Have you brought us—"

A shattering blast exploded.

I screamed.

A bullet had ripped past my head.

8

We sat staring at the neat, round hole in the wall which the bullet had made.

"Sorry," said Willi Thein stiffly. "I—haven't handled a Browning pistol before."

"If *you're* any example of a Czech officer," said Loewy, "no wonder the country fell to the Germans without a shot being fired!"

Suddenly the door was flung open. The mayor stormed into the room. "What kind of crazy men are you? Shooting holes in my guest house! You could easily have shot *me*—the mayor of Balchik!"

"It was—an accident," I said. "We will pay, of course, to have repairs made."

"Yes, you will pay," the mayor shouted. "You will pay plenty!"

We did. Two thousand lei.

The mayor could buy a new guest cabin for that

price. But we needed his help. So we paid his price.

When he left, he invited me to his house for breakfast.

Then I turned to the Ship's Committee. "Tell your passengers that at nine this morning a member of the Mossad will come to the ship to speak to them."

"Impossible!" Alexander exclaimed. "It's against all the rules!"

I knew this, of course. No Mossad leader was to be seen—ever—by the people on the ship. If they did not know who we were—what we looked like—they could not reveal anything. If any of them were caught by the police and questioned—or tortured—they still would say nothing. Because they knew nothing.

It was a wise rule. Remain unknown. But sometimes even the wisest rules must be broken.

I turned to Alexander. "Our people on the ship *must* be made to understand."

"Understand *what?*" said Alexander. "They already know."

"If they did," I said, "no one would be talking about cabling the story of the *Hilda* to the newspapers of the world."

"She is right," said one of the doctors. "We have seven hundred desperate people on board. They must be told what is what. At once. By someone who knows."

66

"How dark is it in the hold?" I asked.

"Like eternal night," said Loewy. "There's no electricity. Only oil lamps for light. And candles."

"Have what light you need for the passengers," I said. "I will stand on a box or a table. In the dark."

"It sounds very dramatic," said Loewy sourly. "The bodiless voice. But what can you *tell* them?"

"I will try to make them understand *their* position," I said slowly. "And our position. And that of the Jews we still hope to save."

Fine words. But what did they mean? What *could* I say to seven hundred men, women, children who had lived for weeks in the hold of a ship which had once been used to carry forty or fifty cows?

The men left to return to the ship. I watched them stomping off through the snow. Then, standing in the doorway, I scooped up some of the white frosty softness and washed my face and hands with it. I wanted to change my clothes and tried to imagine what it must be like to wear the same clothing day and night like the people on the *Hilda*.

I also wanted to take out the scratching envelopes of money. But I could think of no better hiding place. So I left them in my brassiere.

What a fool I'd been to let Willi Thein walk off with both pistols!

What a fool I'd been to promise a bath for seven hundred people. I had no idea at all whether this could be done.

What a fool I had been to break Mossad rules by saying I would come to the ship at nine this morning.

What a fool!

I felt I was drowning in a sea of my own stupidity.

I remembered the words Eliahu had spoken that long-ago day in Tel Aviv when he and Berl Katznelson asked me to become the tenth member of the Mossad. "You'll not only be given a course in swimming," he'd said, "but in life saving."

Life*saving!* But no one had taught me anything about making decisions which could only be called life-and-death. Life or death.

Seven hundred twenty-seven refugees were already aboard the *Hilda*. If I gave orders that the ship should sail as soon as the ice broke, they could reach safety in Palestine. If the ship continued to wait in Balchik harbor, it seemed clear that news of the *Hilda* would reach the authorities in Rumania. Then our ship would be taken. Our people would be sent back to the countries from which they had fled. Fled for their *lives*.

The answer seemed clear enough.

But through the clear answer came the voices sounding in my head. The voices of the children caught in Kladovo. *Wait . . . wait for us.* . . . Two hundred fifty children . . . fifteen hundred human beings. . . . The children spoke for all of them . . . for all of our people trapped in Europe. . . . *Help us.* . . .

And how was I solving problems here in Balchik? With money. Money I had no right to spend. Money which, by contract, we had set aside to give the Shamen if the *Hilda* was taken by the British. It could easily happen. It had happened to other ships.

And here I was promising money as though we had bank vaults of it. Money to bribe the sailors back onto the ship. Money to put the Turkish bath back into working order. Money to buy supplies in Bazargic.

Yet, I did not know any other way to deal with the three mutinies.

First things first. That was a simple rule which Kadmon had taught me. Only it was not so simple. Because it seemed that nothing ever came *first*. Problems came head on. Clashing together. And somehow had to be handled all at the same time.

Yet, now the rule *must* work. I had money with me. People were starving. We must buy food for them. Enough. Finish. Don't think any further!

I went outside.

Icicles hung like daggers from the edge of the roof. The early morning sun was still hidden by clouds. The small houses of the village seemed half buried by snow. Beyond spread the Black Sea. It was well named; black, except at the grayish shoreline. Alexander had told me that the ice trapping our ship was six to eight inches thick.

Should I pray for the ice to melt, so that the *Hilda* could sail for Palestine?

Or should I pray that the ice held so that we would have to wait here for the Kladovo people?

I did not know what to pray for. Yet, I prayed.

"Please, God," I said, "help us."

My words turned to smoke in the cold air.

I entered the mayor's house.

The warmth of the fire was welcoming. So was the mayor's smile.

"Sit down, sit down," he said. And patted the bench beside him.

I sat on the bench across from him.

He poured me a mug of steaming tea.

"Have some bread." He shoved it toward me. Black, thick-crusted, homemade bread. It was very good.

70

"Here." Another shove. White goat cheese and a pot of jam. "My wife is out feeding the animals," the mayor said. Then he smiled. There were two dark gaps where teeth were missing. "It is not often," he added, "that I have such a beauty to join me for breakfast."

I smiled and asked the mayor to please pass the jam.

Instead, he put his hand over mine.

I withdrew my hand to butter the bread which I told him was very good. "Did your wife make this?"

He did not answer.

I could not risk making him angry. "I—need your advice," I said. (I had found in the past that a father-daughter approach worked well, even though a man had other matters on his mind.)

"I am grateful," I said, "to have so wise a person to turn to."

He leaned back in his chair, and leaned right into the father role. "How can I help you, my dear."

I told him that the people on our ship would have nothing left to eat in a few days time. And, since I had money, the mayor agreed to get together a group of men who would drive empty sleighs to Bazargic. Alexander, Arkadi, and I would go along as "buying agents."

"But I must warn you, my dear," the mayor said.

71

"This area—the Dobrudja—is known for its thieves and smugglers. If you drive off with all that money —" He said no more. But his face said it all.

"Would it help if Alexander and Arkadi each carried a gun?"

"Help?" the mayor exploded. "If they handle a gun as well as your friend in the cabin, yes it would help. It would help those who may attack you and take your guns from you!"

Since there seemed no more to say on that subject, I passed on to another one. The matter of the Turkish bath.

Again, the mayor exploded. "Impossible!" He repeated the word, accenting each syllable. "IM-POSS-IBLE! That Turkish bath has not been used for eighty years! We could never heat it. And the wells up there have been dry since the day of the death of the King's mother, God rest her soul."

"Couldn't water be carried up there, in barrels?"

"Have you seen that Turkish bath?" cried the mayor. "It's on the top of a steep hill. You might even call it a cliff. Look," he said, "your people have gone without a bath for weeks. Let them stink for a few weeks longer."

I tried to make him understand that they were on the edge of despair and desperation. "I believe," I said quietly, "that this bath can do more to raise their spirits than any other single thing. Except—setting off for Palestine."

"Ah! And just when *do* you plan to sail?"

"As soon as the ice breaks."

"No more waiting for more people who never arrive?"

"No more waiting."

There. I had said it. I had made the decision—without meaning to. Was it the right decision? What would happen to the Kladovo people if we left? But what would happen to the people on the *Hilda* if we did not leave? A cable from the mayor of Balchik to the police in Bucharest—and the ship would be doomed. All its passengers would be sent back to the countries they'd fled from.

Perhaps the visas for the Kladovo people would come through before the ice broke. It was my hope, my prayer. It *must* happen. I would phone Sima Spitzer from Bazargic and tell him the situation. He had already made superhuman efforts to get the visas. Now he must try even harder.

By the end of our breakfast the mayor had agreed to try to get a group of the strongest men in town to carry barrels of water up to the Turkish bath. I was sure that he would succeed—since each of these men would be paid more than he could earn in a week during the wintertime.

I left the mayor's house, feeling that some of the ship's problems would be solved.

But the biggest problem lay ahead.

Dealing with the passengers.

This was something I had to handle alone. Money could not help me here. Nothing would help. Except words. My words to them. And I had no idea at all what I should say.

The bitter cold of the early morning hit me as I walked down the steep path. But it was nothing compared to the cold I felt deep inside. I was frozen—by fear.

9

At nine o'clock I walked up the ice-slick gangplank of the *Hilda*.

Alexander was waiting on deck. There was no one else around.

"They're all below," Alexander said, taking my arm. "The stage is set. But I don't like the mood of the audience."

We bent into the strong sea wind. When we came to the doorway leading down to the hold, Alexander said, "Good luck. You'll need it."

Then he disappeared.

I followed him down the ladder. The darkness stank of sweat and vomit.

Alexander lifted me onto a packing case.

Waves of bodies swelled before me. Some sat. Some squatted, or stood. The rest lay on berths—a slab of wood with two feet between it and the wooden board above. There was not room for a person to sit up straight. But the more such berths we built in the hold of each of our secret ships, the more people we could carry to safety.

The portholes were open. Circles of daylight fell on some of the faces. Others were lit by the pale glow from kerosene lamps.

I stood in darkness.

"What's he like?" someone called out.

"It's a *woman*. A little—nobody!" The voice was sharp with scorn.

"*Shalom*," I said. The word with three meanings. *Hello. Good-by.* And *peace.*

The people before me were far from peaceful. Their silence was alive with hatred.

It was like waking suddenly to find men and women of your nightmare turned into real human beings. Women with matted, uncombed hair. Dark-bearded men; angry, threatening.

My mind blanked. There were no words.

Their voices rose.

"For God's sake, talk to them!" Alexander said.

"*Haverim* . . . comrades."

"Louder!" Alexander said.

"*Haverim!*" My voice rang out through the stinking gloom. "I have been sent here by the Mossad. We have met with your Ship's Committee. We will try to help in every way that we can. We know your

76

problems. But you must try to understand *our* problems. And the problems of those who will—God willing—come after you. On ships like this one. Or worse than this one. Because"—I took a deep breath—"because their fate is in your hands."

I paused. No one spoke. But their anger was so solid I could almost touch it, like a wall.

I told them all that I could—perhaps more than I should—about what we were trying to do. I told them about the impossibilities of our job. To find ships. Impossible, since the outbreak of the war when every nation needed ships. And *their* needs were called "legal." Ours were called "illegal."

When we *did* find a ship—even an old leaky cargo ship like the *Hilda*—there was only one way to get the owner to let us have it. We must offer more money than any of the other people who wanted the ship.

And this was another impossibility. Getting the money. Every Jewish organization in the world was, at that time, against illegal immigration. With one exception. The Histadrut. The labor union in Palestine. They had given us money. But I hated to think where it came from. The workers' sick fund. The old-age fund.

The leaders of the Histadrut believed—as we did—that the Jews of Europe were on the road to doom.

And the people on this ship believed it. If they did

not, they would not be here. They would not have fled from their homes, leaving everything behind them. The street they lived on. The school their children went to. The shops they knew. Leaving their friends, their relatives. Leaving their life behind them. For what? To try to reach a homeland they had never seen. Palestine. Where they would have to learn a new language. Find a new life. Palestine— where they would still be in danger. In danger of arrest by the British. In danger of being murdered during Arab riots.

Yet, Palestine also meant a chance for a normal life. And, as Jews, they knew they could not find this in Hitler's Europe.

They knew. They all came from countries overtaken by Hitler.

But Jews in other countries still thought themselves safe. And because no one believed in what we were doing, they would not give us money. A fly-by-night group, they called us. Risking people's lives on our leaky old ships. Ships that could be blown up by a mine in the Mediterranean.

I told the people in the hold of the *Hilda* how hard it was to raise money for our secret ships. And why. "Yet," I said, my voice rising into the gloom, "we will spend the little money we have to buy the food that you need. And to buy you a bath." I told them the plans for getting the Turkish bath in working order.

They seemed at least to be listening now, without anger.

Then I said what was most on my mind. Perhaps I said it too soon.

I told them there must be no more talk of cabling their story to the newspapers of the free world.

"Why not?" someone shouted out. "The story would make the front pages. *That's* what we want! To open the eyes of the world! Let them know what's going on here. What's happening to the Jews of Europe."

Voices swelled. Agreeing. Yelling. Angry again.

"YES!" I shouted to be heard above them. "The front pages. That's where your story *should* appear!"

Again, quiet. They wanted to hear me agree with them.

"Yes," I repeated. "You're right. Your story would make good newspaper copy. A shipload of men, women, children. Guilty of nothing. Yet, forced to flee from their homes. Trapped here on a ship. Desperate. Starving. Yes, your story *should* appear on the front pages of newspapers. In America. In England. In France. In Switzerland. It should appear there. But *would* it? What happened to the story of the Evian Conference? How was *that* covered by the newspapers? Have you heard of the Evian Conference?"

Some murmured yes. Some said no. Most said nothing.

"That was a story more dramatic than yours," I told them. "It was one of the greatest news stories of the century. And the reporters were there. Top reporters from thirty-two countries."

"What *was* Evian?" A woman's voice came shrill from the darkness. "I never heard of this Evian Conference."

"It took place a year before the war broke out," I said. "In July 1938. High officials from thirty-two countries met in the French resort town of Evian. Beautiful Evian on Lake Geneva. Why did they meet? For one reason. To see what they could do to help the Jews of Germany and Austria. For one week the delegates heard eyewitness reports. From people like you. Reports about what was going on right then in Germany and Austria. What was happening to the Jews. You remember what was happening. It was happening to you.

"The delegates were given facts, figures. By 1937 half the Jews in Germany had been fired from their jobs. Fired and unable to find other work. Fired for one reason only. They were Jews. The delegates were told about the signs: hanging above hotel doorways . . . in shop windows . . . in public parks . . . movie houses . . . swimming pools. NO JEWS ALLOWED. Even above the kindergartens, signs. JEWISH SCUM. The delegates were told that in some towns a Jew could not buy milk for his children. Or medicine. Or groceries. Because of the signs. NO JEWS.

"The delegates were told—by eyewitnesses— what had happened when German troops marched into Austria, and took it over. In a single day. You remember that day. March 12, 1938. Four months before the Evian Conference. The delegates were told that within a few weeks tens of thousands of Austrian Jews had been locked up in concentration camps. How many of your friends, relatives, were among those thousands?

"The delegates were told how Jewish men, women, even small children were beaten up on the streets by black-booted soldiers, while Austrians stood around watching, cheering, jeering. A Jewish housewife told the delegates how she had been on the way to the store, when she was stopped by soldiers. Forced down on her hands and knees to scrub the gutter. She showed them her hands, burned raw. Because acid had been added to the scrub water. An old rabbi told the delegates how he had been sent to scrub out the public toilets. On and on the reports went. The horror stories.

"And the delegates were read the words Hitler had shouted. 'If the Jews of Europe again make a World War, the result will be—the wiping out of the Jewish race in Europe!'

"Then the delegates were told a surprising fact, which few of them knew. Jews—whom Hitler blamed for every evil—were only *one per cent* of the German population. Only 3 *per cent* of the Austrian population. At the time of the Evian Conference there were only 350,000 Jews left in Germany. Only 190,000 Jews in Austria.

"Now among the nations who came to Evian were some of the largest countries in the world. In each of these countries there were miles upon miles upon miles of land—with no one living on it. Canada was one of the thirty-two nations at Evian. Canada: the second-largest country in the world. Brazil, the fifth-largest. Australia, the sixth-largest. And in all of Australia—an entire continent—there were only as many people as there are in the city of London. Those three countries—and many others at the Evian conference—needed people. Needed workers. Any one of them could have taken every Jewish man, woman and child in Germany and Austria.

"Well, how many did they agree to take?" This

time the silence was stiff. I felt I could reach out my hand and smash it.

They were waiting. But I could not speak. Tears clogged my throat.

"Tell us."

"What happened?"

Several men in the packed crowd stood up. Shouted at me.

"*What happened at Evian?*"

"TELL US WHAT HAPPENED."

Others took up the cry. Voices swelled through the hold. The sound was so loud it seemed it would shove back the wooden walls.

10

I held up my hands for quiet. But since I stood in the dark, they did not see me.

Finally, Alexander shouted: *"If you want to hear, let her speak!"*

When they had quieted again, my voice returned. Words came. Low. Slow. If I did not keep them this way, the words might have sounded like a scream.

"Nations of asylum. That is what they called themselves—these thirty-two countries. It was a fine title. Asylum. Look it up in the dictionary. Asylum. The first meaning listed: place of retreat and security. Place of refuge. And that's why they had come to Evian, these thirty-two nations. To offer a place of refuge and security. In fact, never before in history had this happened. Nations of the world gathering for the one and only purpose of saving a doomed people. Never before in history had it happened."

I paused.

They waited.

"Well," I said, "you asked the question, 'what happened?' I will tell you. On the last day of the Evian Conference each delegate stood up to tell what his country could do. To help. For a week they had listened to the facts, figures, eyewitness reports. It had been made very clear that it was a life-or-death matter. The Jews of Germany and Austria were desperate to get out. *But they had to have someplace to go!*

"The first delegate to speak on the last day was Ambassador Myron C. Taylor from the United States. Everyone listened hard to what *he* had to say! Why? Because the United States President— Franklin D. Roosevelt—was the man who had called this conference. It was his idea. His country would lead the way. Or so everyone thought.

"But Myron C. Taylor told the delegates that— unfortunately—the United States had its quota system. A certain number of people were allowed in from each country, each year. Do you know what the quota is for Rumania, for instance—the country in which we are now sitting? Two hundred eighty-nine. Two hundred eighty-nine Rumanians allowed into the United States each year. You've heard the story about the Rumanian Jew who went into the United

States embassy in Bucharest to ask for a visa? He was told to come back in the year 2003. 'In the morning,' he asked, 'or in the afternoon?'"

No one laughed. The "joke" was too hard for humor.

"Myron C. Taylor explained the United States quota system. He explained why there was nothing his country could do. Then he sat down.

"This was the help offered by the nation made up of immigrants! The nation which, through its history, had offered—asylum. This was the answer the United States gave at Evian—a closed door. Ambassador Taylor knew, however, that there were many others who would take the Jews of Germany and Austria. There were, after all, thirty-one nations to be heard from.

"Canada? The delegate explained that his country could only accept farmers. It had, of course, been clearly brought out at the Evian Conference that Jews in Germany and Austria were forbidden by law to be farmers. There *was* no such thing as a Jewish farmer!

"It turned out that four other countries also had that same rule. Only farmers wanted.

"Brazil—huge Brazil—had a brand-new law. No one could come into Brazil without a certificate of baptism. You had to be a Christian to get into Brazil!

"Australia? The delegate announced that they had no racial problem there—and did not want to 'import' one!

"Four large South American countries listed intellectuals and merchants as—guess what? *Undesirables!* Of course, half the Jews in Germany and Austria are intellectuals: doctors, lawyers, teachers, other such—types. Most of the rest are businessmen. Merchants.

"And so it went. All through the last day of the Conference. One delegate after the other—with the same message. It was certainly a terrible time now for Jews in Germany and Austria. They clearly needed help. It was too bad, but *his* country had certain rules. So *his* country could do nothing to help. But surely there were many other countries which would welcome the half million German and Austrian Jews.

"There were three. Three of the smallest nations at the conference. Holland—Jews could flee there and stay till they found a home somewhere else. Denmark—would take fifteen hundred. The Dominican Republic would take more—if they agreed to be Jews no longer.

"But even these three countries voted for the final resolution. *All* of the thirty-two nations of asylum voted for it. What *was* the resolution? No Jews would be taken in unless they brought their money with them. They had to be able to support themselves. Of course *you* well know that no Jew is allowed *out* of Germany or Austria with more than ten *Reichsmarks*. Less than five dollars. You know it. And every delegate at Evian knew it! It had been clearly brought out at the Conference.

"So by that one resolution they made every Jew in Germany and Austria unacceptable to"—I choked on the words—"the nations of asylum!"

Through the silence in the hold I heard the soft sound of weeping.

Finally I said, "The reporters were there at Evian. Reporters from thirty-two nations. This was a story! One of the biggest stories of our century. Did it make the headlines in newspapers all over the world? I'll tell you what happened. On the opening day of that historic conference, the great New York *Times* ran a small story about it on page thirteen. They gave twice the space that same day to the news that Adolf Hitler had visited an art show.

"Now what about the last day? The day that one nation after the other said that they could do nothing to help the Jews of Germany and Austria. They had come to Evian to offer help. But all they had done was turn their backs. Locked the doors. That was a news story, was it not?

"Well, the New York *Times* did not think so. The

story they ran was even smaller than the first. And they ran it on page twenty."

Again I paused, because I wanted to scream the sentence. But I did not. I said the words in a normal tone. But the words held their own scream.

"The New York *Times* was one of the few newspapers in the world to print any Evian stories at all."

"The story of the *Hilda* might also be used on page twenty of the New York *Times*. Will that make the people of the world run to help you? I'll tell you what would happen. Rumanian police would come here at once. They would take over our ship. You would all be sent back to the countries you came from. And the Mossad would be—finished. We could save no more people. Is that what you're after?"

This time silence was an answer; the answer I wanted.

We were partners now, the people on this ship and the Mossad. We were together, because they understood now that we were all alone.

"When will we sail?" someone asked.

"When the ice breaks."

"No more waiting for the Kladovo people?"

"The mayor told me," I said, "that if we do not get out when the ice breaks, he will tell to police in Bucharest that our ship is here."

"You must get the pregnant women off," someone shouted from the back.

"Yes!" Another voice, a shout. "If you don't, you'll be murderers. No infant could live in this hellhole."

"Yes! Get them off!"

The words became a roar. They all agreed. Get them off the ship. Now.

A woman got to her feet. A kerosene lamp hung close to her body. Her swollen body.

Silence fell around her.

"And if you put us off the ship, will my baby live? Or will it one day soon be killed by strangers?" Her voice rose. "If my baby dies I would rather have it die on this ship of Jews. Headed for the homeland." She turned to me. "Please. Don't put us off the ship. Please, God, let us stay!"

She had called upon God. Words came into my head. Words from the Bible. I said them aloud. "The Lord said to his prophet Jeremiah, 'Arise ye, and let us go up to Zion. . . . Behold I will bring them from the north country . . . the blind and the lame and the woman with child. . . .'"

I paused.

Then I knew I need say no more. Not about this.

She knew it too—the woman with child.

"Thank you," she said. And she sat down.

I repeated her words. "Thank you. Thank all of you. You are all heroes. No one will give you medals. But you must know inside you—every one of you is a hero. Every Jew who struggles and suffers to keep alive . . . is a hero. You are—our tomorrow."

I climbed down from the wooden crate on which I stood.

Hands reached for me; led me to the ladder.

Someone started singing "Hatikvah." Our national anthem. The national anthem of a people. A people without a country, except one given to them by God. *Hatikvah,* the ancient Hebrew word meaning *hope.*

I climbed up the iron ladder into the sudden brightness of the morning.

11

A few hours later we set out for Bazargic.

There were ten sleighs, each with a driver. Otherwise each was empty.

The mayor had told the drivers that we were going to pick up more people for our ship. "If I let them know you were going to buy food," the mayor told me, "you might be killed before you got to Bazargic. Food to fill up ten sleighs means you must be carrying money. A lot of money. More money than any of my people have seen in a lifetime. Money like that can mean murder—on an empty road."

I sat in the first sleigh next to Alexander. We had left Arkadi in Balchik. His job was to find the sailors. Some of them had now taken up with girls of the town. Arkadi, therefore, had to enter each of the small mud-brick houses in Balchik. Many of these homes had only one room, with an outhouse in the back, and a shed for animals. Still, they were warm. Which the ship was not. And there were other attractions.

It was no easy job to get each sailor to leave the house. Leave the girl. Come back to the ship. Go to work. Money did not always speak loudly enough. Not even the offer of one hundred pounds sterling.

But money had spoken loudly enough when it came to the Turkish bath.

In the distance, tiny figures inched their way up the snow-crusted hill. Each carried a wooden barrel on his back. They were, the mayor had told us, the twelve strongest men in the village. If they could not get the Turkish bath in working order, it could not be done.

As we drove through Balchik the barking dogs came running across the ice and snow to snarl and snap at the horses. But in the morning sunlight, the dogs did not seem so fearsome as they had when they "greeted us" the night before.

In fact, everything now seemed more hopeful.

Our *Hilda* passengers had started up their committees again. There was a Work Committee, a Fire Brigade, a Clean-Up Committee, a Lecture Committee, a Committee to Teach Hebrew, a Hanukkah Committee to prepare a program for the holiday which was coming soon. And there was a Captain's Cabin

Committee. Arkadi had bribed the captain to let us use his cabin as a hospital room. Here the two babies would be born.

People collected buckets of snow, to be boiled. Then they scrubbed and cleaned the filthy cabin.

I had promised to buy sheets and other things the doctors would need—if they could be found in Bazargic.

We reached the town in the late afternoon.

Despite the mounds of blankets which covered us, we were half frozen. We could have done with a hot drink at the village pub. But time seemed to be nipping at our heels like the half-wild village dogs.

We left the drivers at the pub. I ran to the post office. There—and only there—could I make a long-distance telephone call.

The man who sold stamps behind the grilled window was also in charge of the telephone. When I put in my "order" he stared at me. His mouth fell open. "You say that you want to phone Switzerland. Greece. Turkey. Yugoslavia. And Palestine?"

I nodded. "Yes. All urgent calls."

"You think this is the telephone exchange in Bucharest?" he shouted at me. "It would take me a week to get all those calls through. And then you'd

95

be lucky if you could hear a word from the other end."

"Well—try Yugoslavia," I told him. "Just that one. It's a matter of life and death."

"Oh yes," he said. "Life and death. Of course. Of course. You have a lover in Yugoslavia. Is that it?"

"No, that is not it."

I *must* reach Sima Spitzer. I must tell him that our ship would have to leave when the ice broke. Had his visas come through? If the Kladovo people were on the way, even if they could leave today—tomorrow— surely the mayor of Balchik would allow our ship to wait in the harbor. I had to know about the visas. And Spitzer had to know what was happening about the *Hilda*.

But how could I tell this to the fat-faced man behind the grilled window?

He smiled at me. His teeth were yellow. "If I try —very hard," he said slowly, "I might be able to get a call through in a few hours time."

He did not say the words, but I heard them. *If you pay more money.*

I nodded. I took a hundred lei from my pocket- book. I looked behind me. The post office was empty.

I pushed the money through the grilled window.

In return he gave me the back of an old envelope, the stub of a pencil. "Write down your number," he said. "Then sit. And wait. I promise you nothing except that I will try."

Alexander meanwhile was out buying food and supplies.

What would our ten drivers do when they learned we had tricked them? We had not, after all, come here to pick up more people.

Would they turn on us, in anger. After a few hours in the pub would it be drunken anger?

Would Arkadi be able to get the seamen back to the ship?

Would the captain be able to keep them there until the ice broke?

Would the two babies be born alive? *Should* I have brought the two women to the hospital in Bazargic?

Would the visas come through on time?

Would the call come through?

Would Spitzer be there?

Questions—all manner of questions—hammered at me as I sat on the wooden bench in the post office.

Two hours later Alexander burst in.

His cheeks and nose were red with cold.

"Well," he said, "we're ready to go. I've bought

out the town. The sleighs are loaded. The drivers are waiting."

I stood up. "How can I go? I haven't reached Spitzer. I haven't even been able to get a call through to Bucharest."

The man behind the window shrugged and gave me his yellow smile. "I tried my best. You know that I tried."

"We can't wait any longer," Alexander said. "The sun's going down. The drivers will start to freeze."

So I left with Alexander.

But as I walked from the post office, I seemed to hear their voices. *Wait for us. Wait.* The Kladovo people. Was I going mad? *Please wait for us.* The shrill, clear voices of the children. The two hundred fifty children.

The sleighs were piled high with crates and sacks. Alexander told me what he had bought: coffee, sugar, tea, rice, cereals, biscuits, hard cheese, candles, soap, and carton upon carton of canned goods. There were also medicines of various sorts. And a sheet for each of the beds in the captain's cabin.

"I tried to buy diapers," Alexander said. "And little shirts. They have nothing here for newborn babies."

"What did the drivers say when they saw all this?" I asked him. "Were they angry?"

"I told them we'd pay their bill at the pub. That made them forget everything else."

The drivers sang drunkenly and laughed and called to each other. None of them seemed in fit condition to drive a loaded sleigh over ice-slick roads.

I was certain that we would end up in a snowbank.

But somehow we made it safely back to Balchik.

That night the people from our ship and from the town watched and cheered as supplies we had bought in Bazargic were brought aboard the ship.

And that night two babies were born in the captain's cabin. A girl and a boy.

The girl was born first. Her parents named her Hilda.

The boy was given a Hebrew name. Yehuda.

The Hebrew word for Jew.

12

The two babies seemed to bring new hope to the people on the ship.

Even the crew members felt that the babies were a sign of good luck. They came back to the ship. They went to work.

By noon the cooks were serving a large hot meal; the first in many weeks.

All this was reported to me by Alexander and Arkadi. I did not dare return to the ship myself. I had broken enough rules already. There was no need any longer for me to go on board the *Hilda*.

In fact, now that all seemed to be going well, I decided to go back to Bucharest. There I would sit by the phone until I reached Sima Spitzer.

As I got ready to leave, a peasant woman came to see me in the mayor's house.

"Here," she said. "For the babies. I heard that

they had no diapers." And she handed me a pile of hand-stitched folded diapers. "I made them," she said with a shy smile. "I made them from sheets and a tablecloth I was saving for my—wedding chest."

I looked at her. Then suddenly I could not see her. My eyes had filled with tears.

When a peasant woman was past her twenties, it was often hard to tell her age. Was this woman giving away her final hopes of marriage by cutting up the sheets she had saved for her own wedding? Or had those hopes been packed away long ago with the unused linens?

"It's very kind of you," I said. "Maybe you'd like to go on board yourself—and give this present to the mothers."

She shook her head. "No, please. I don't want that. Just tell the two mothers—I wish them well. And I bless the babies. May they have a good life."

Then, before I could stop her, she pulled her dark shawl over her hair. And she hurried out the door.

I stood staring after her. And I wondered why her simple human act had moved me to tears.

I had not cried at what I saw on the *Hilda*. Human beings living for seven weeks in the stinking, filthy, crowded hold. Human beings, half starved, half frozen. Each given the amount of sleeping space he would get in a grave.

I had not cried at the reports I'd heard—the hundreds of horror stories. Jewish families torn apart. A father, a brother, sometimes a mother, even a child —taken off by German soldiers. Never heard from again.

To keep going, one had to learn not to cry. When it came to what was happening to the Jews—one could not cry. Otherwise one would cry all the time.

But to go on as a human being, tears had to come sometimes.

Tears could come at the kindness of a peasant woman who cut up her wedding sheets to make a gift of diapers.

I left Balchik several hours later.

The mayor's son would take me part way by sleigh.

I would stay overnight in a pub. Then, in the morning, I would—I hoped—make my way on to Bucharest.

Alexander and Arkadi wanted to come with me. "A girl like you," Alexander said, "alone for hours with one of these—"

"Wild men!" Arkadi said.

I too was frightened at the idea of taking the trip alone. But the two men were needed here in Balchik.

"No one will bother me," I said. "It's much too cold."

Alexander gave a shout of laughter. "The cold weather will be your body guard, Ruth?"

"I'll be all right," I said. I sounded far more certain than I felt.

As I left Balchik I heard singing. A Hebrew song! The words came clear through the frosty afternoon.

The mayor's son pointed up to the Turkish bath.

One line of people made their way up the steep hill. Others came downhill, singing.

They were singing because they were clean.

They had soaped and soaked themselves. They had washed their clothes. Back on the ship they had strung up clothes lines on the deck. Drying skirts, shirts, trousers, were flapping in the winter wind. I had the feeling they were waving me a cheerful good-by.

As it turned out, the sleigh drivers on my trip back caused me no trouble at all. However, I very nearly killed myself—in the car Alexander had rented. I am not much of a driver in the best of cars, on the best of roads, in the best of weather.

How I managed to get back home driving—skidding—on ice-slick roads, in a thumping old car in the middle of the night, is still a mystery.

I walked into my room, shaken, shaking. I had been away three days. It seemed like three months.

I went straight to the telephone.

When the call to Spitzer finally came through, it was as though I had never left. His words were the same as they'd always been. "You must wait. One more—two more days at the most. I will surely have the visas by then."

I told him that when the ice broke, the *Hilda* would sail. There was no other way.

Spitzer started screaming at me.

Then there was swift silence. Either the connection had been cut. Or Spitzer had hung up on me.

I phoned Moshe. It was two in the morning. His daughter, Rita, answered the phone. She was a pretty child, twelve years old. "Who is it?" she asked sleepily.

"I'm sorry I woke you," I said. "Is your daddy at home?"

"He didn't come home yet," Rita said. "He's at some meeting."

Did the child feel the same fear that I did? Did she know the danger in which her father lived? Danger because he worked with us: the Mossad. The Mossad with its illegal activities: saving human lives.

"Would you leave a note for him, Rita? Have him call me when he comes in. My name is Ruth."

"I know," she said. "I know your voice. I'll give him the message."

She hung up.

Was he at a meeting? Or was he in prison?

I peeled off my layers of clothing. I left puddles of them, lying on the floor. And I got into bed.

Dreams ripped my sleep. Dreams and voices. Voices of the Kladovo children. Little children trapped on a river boat in the Danube. "Each has one thin blanket," Spitzer had told me. "Their feet are swollen with frostbite. They are starving."

Why were they there? Because they were Jews. But *why?* Because they were Jews. The answer did not fit the question. Yet, it *was* the answer. Just because they were Jews. It could not be the answer. There *was* no answer. There was only the question. *Why?* It filled the room: louder. LOUDER.

WHY?

And through the question came the cries of the children. *Don't leave. Don't leave us here.*

At four in the morning the phone rang.

I jumped from nightmare sleep. "Yes?"

It was Moshe.

"Thank God," I said.

He had, in fact, been with the police. They had broken into his office. They had pulled out his files. Cards lay all over the floor. Each card held the name of a human being begging for a certificate. A legal certificate of entry to Palestine.

Moshe Orekhovsky was the man in charge of *legal* immigration to Palestine. In charge of the Palestine Office. Every day he received hundreds of applications for certificates. And every month he received from the British Mandatory Government, ten, sometimes twelve, legal certificates of entry to Palestine.

Then Moshe Orekhovsky had to play God. Which of the thousands of names in his file should be given these few legal certificates?

And what could he offer the others?

That was why he had joined with us: the Mossad.

"Perhaps," he could say to the desperate people who came to him, or wrote to him, "perhaps I can find a way to get you on one of the *illegal* ships."

No one knew how many of the "secret ships" there were. No one knew from where they sailed, or how many they could save. Our ships, therefore, could at least offer hope. And it was this hope which was giving thousands of Jews a rope to pull themselves out of the swamp of despair.

"The police kept me with them for six hours,"

Moshe told me. "They were looking for proof that I was working with the Mossad. But they found nothing. So they let me go. *This* time," he added.

"Maybe you should—" I broke off. I needed him. We all needed him. But his little girl Rita needed him too. His child and his wife.

He finished my question. "Maybe I should cut loose from you? Yes . . . maybe I should. But—how can I? When I get to the office in the morning, they are sitting on the steps, filling the hallways. People begging for certificates. They come even to my house to ask for certificates. I have no peace. My wife has no peace." His voice changed suddenly. "Ruth, the *Hilda?* What happened? How are things there? Will the ship sail?"

I told him briefly. And then I said, "The reason I phoned—if the visas for the Kladovo people do not come through . . . Moshe, we'll have room for more people on the *Hilda.* Maybe one hundred more. We must get them to Balchik. The *Hilda* is ready to sail as soon as the ice breaks. We must take as many as we can. And I don't think—the Kladovo people— Perhaps we will find another ship for the Kladovo people."

"Yes," Moshe said. "Maybe . . . another ship."

But we both knew there was little or no hope of finding another ship.

"You are right," he said then. "You must take the people who are free to go. I will contact one hundred of them in the morning."

I hung up suddenly.

I could speak no more.

What would happen to them now? Fifteen hundred men, women, children trapped on a river boat on the Danube. Trapped because they could not get visas to cross a country in a sealed train.

13

Moshe chose one hundred people for the *Hilda*. But they did not all leave at once. They had to go as we had done, by horse and sleigh. No more than twenty could be taken there each day.

I did not tell Spitzer that other people were filling the berths we had saved for the Kladovo people. But every day we spoke on the phone. "You must try harder," I told him. "I know you are doing everything. But do more than everything!"

If the visas came through we could still get some of his people onto our ship. Other Mossad ships, filled solid with people, had been forced to take on more. Some had stopped in mid-sea to take on all the people from another illegal ship—which was sinking.

The winter weather began to ease. The ice would break soon. The *Hilda* would have to leave. When it did, Spitzer would lose all chance for *any* visas.

On the first week of the new year, Alexander came back to Bucharest.

I'd heard nothing from him, nothing of the *Hilda* since I left Balchik.

He had much to tell me. Too much.

"You left," he said, "on the Day of the Turkish Bath. That was the *Hilda*'s happy day. Her one happy day."

He then told me about the fire.

On the afternoon of December 29, someone had accidentally filled the kerosene lamps with benzene. One of our people lit a lamp. It blazed up. He threw it from him. The benzene fell on the clothes of a woman. The lamp fell on straw, used as a mattress. Flames blazed up. In a few moments the fire climbed to other straw mattresses. The hold became a blazing hell.

Panic broke out, wild as the flames.

People ran for the ladder, screaming, shoving.

The woman with benzene on her clothes was accidentally shoved into the fire. Her clothes flamed. People tore them off. She was carried, moaning, up to the deck.

The fire brigade somehow managed to put out the flames. But many had been badly burned. The woman who had been set afire screamed in pain for two days. Then she died.

Her name was Irmagard Levinstein. For two years she had been training for the life she would live on a kibbutz in Palestine.

The day after the fire, the ice started to break up.

Alexander told me that he had planned to travel to Bazargic. He wanted to let me know. Let Spitzer know. But he could not leave Balchik. A terrible winter storm broke out on the Black Sea.

Alexander was aboard the *Hilda* when the anchors were torn loose.

"It was horrible," he told me. "We had the feeling that all the forces of hell came together to toss our ship from side to side."

Wind had cracked the ship against the pier, then drove it out to the open sea.

"We rang sirens for help," Alexander said. "But no one heard us. We knew that no one would hear. We could barely hear the sirens ourselves. Because of the noise of the storm.

"We were afraid of fire. So we put out the fire in the ovens. We put out all the lamps. We were in pitch blackness. All of us—prisoned in that black hold. Everyone seasick. The shrieking wind. The moaning. The vomiting. The stinking darkness.

Never in any dream could I make up such a nightmare. We were all sure the ship would sink."

"What—happened?" My words were so soft I could hardly hear them.

"The next morning the storm let up. We got back to Balchik. The ship was leaking badly. Repairs had to be made."

I sat down, weak. "And the people on board?"

"No one died. Everyone thought we all would. But—we survived." Alexander grinned. "In fact, we even celebrated Hanukkah." And he told me about it. Tears came to my eyes.

The Hanukkah Committee had built a huge wooden candelabra. And the *Hilda* passengers joined with Jews throughout the world as they celebrated the Feast of Lights. They sang the songs, and they told the stories. Songs and stories from centuries of the Jewish past.

Then a young man and a girl who had met on the ship stood up and announced their engagement.

A few days later we received a cable from Arkadi.

Fishermen had found the *Hilda*'s anchors. All the repairs had been made. And our ship—with 729 people on board—had sailed for Palestine.

I did not tell Spitzer. Not yet. If his visas came through and the fifteen hundred Kladovo people were at least allowed to cross Bulgaria and get to a Black Sea port . . .

Then what?

A question with no answer.

Maybe somehow we could find a ship. Maybe somewhere . . . Some miracle . . .

But where, how, to house fifteen hundred people. People with nowhere to go—except Palestine. And no way to get to Palestine.

Perhaps I did not phone Spitzer right away because I could not face his anger, his despair.

For twenty-four hours we heard nothing at all about the *Hilda*. Then, finally, a telephone call came from our Mossad man in Istanbul.

The ship had put into port to take on more coal. That was according to plan. And, also according to plan, all our people had been asked to hide in the hold while the ship was in port.

Except in cases of emergency—like this one—there were always some passengers on deck. Even in rain, or snow. It had to be this way. The hold had been built to carry perhaps fifty cows. Seven hundred twenty-nine people could not be jammed in that space for more than an hour or so at a time. It was impossible.

But in Istanbul the impossible was necessary.

If British spies saw the illegals, the *Hilda* might just as well turn around and head back to Rumania. And there were hundreds of British spies. They came in all nationalities.

So, in Istanbul, our people stayed below. And goats roamed free on deck. Goats had been taken aboard at Balchik for milk. Also, so that the captain could claim that his ship was carrying farm animals.

But that night in the port at Istanbul, sickness spread suddenly in the hold. The toilets were all on deck. Hoping that they would be covered by darkness, men and women had crept up on deck. They stood in long lines at the toilets. They leaned on deck rails to vomit into the sea.

They were seen.

As the ship left the harbor, searchlights were turned on her. The *Hilda* was flooded with brightness.

Two British Royal Navy ships sandwiched the *Hilda* between them. A British officer and two crewmen came on board our ship. And took it over.

That night a young girl jumped overboard. They brought her back, screaming and sobbing. It was the same girl who had tried to kill herself when the *Hilda* was caught in the ice in Balchik.

Then the *Hilda*, still between the two British ships, had sailed off. And she had not been seen since.

We made frantic phone calls to Turkey. To Greece. To Palestine. What had happened to the *Hilda?* No one knew. Could a ship simply disappear?

Finally, on January 24, a cable came from Palestine. Two British ships were bringing the *Hilda* into Haifa harbor.

What did it mean?

Moshe was with me when the cable came. I stared at him. "Maybe now—in the fifth month of the war —the British have finally understood who their friends really are in Palestine."

"Maybe," Moshe said. He did not sound hopeful.

It was unbelievable. On the one hand the British were our heroes. They were fighting Hitler. On the other hand, the British were our enemy. They ruled in Palestine. They ruled because in 1917 the British had put out the Balfour Declaration. This backed the idea of a national home for the Jewish people in Palestine. And they promised to do all they could to help the Jews win this goal.

Because of this Balfour Declaration, the League of Nations had given Britain a "mandate" to rule in Palestine.

But since they'd become the rulers of Palestine in 1922, the British had done nothing at all to help the Jews in their dream for a new Jewish country in the ancient Jewish homeland.

In fact, the British had done what they could to destroy the dream. And in May 1939, less than four months before the start of World War II, the British had put out a White Paper. With one cold sentence it wiped out all the promises of the Balfour Declaration: "His Majesty's Government now declare that it is *not* part of their policy that Palestine should become a Jewish state."

Why? The reason was clear enough. The Arabs did not want a Jewish state in Palestine. The Arabs had oil. With war coming, Britain needed Arab oil more than ever. And needed the friendship of the Arab countries.

So the British put out their White Paper—which said that for the next five years there would be only 817 legal certificates each month for all the Jews of all the world who wished to come to Palestine.

Of these, Moshe Orekhovsky was given ten or twelve a month.

Millions of European Jews were desperate to get to Palestine. And the British were doing all that they could to make sure that the Jews would not get in.

Our secret ships had to land people on a lonely beach, on a moonless night.

Many of our ships had been caught by the British. Then one of three things happened. The people were landed and sent to Atlit Detention Camp: a prison. Their numbers were then subtracted from the quota of legal certificates put out the next month. Or, the people were sent back to the countries they had fled from. Or, the ships were sent out to sea without food, water, fuel. They were never heard from again.

Unbelievable.

Even so, most of the young Jews in Palestine had volunteered to fight with the British Army. They were rejected. We had heard of no Arabs who volunteered to fight with the British Army. In fact, the Grand Mufti, the most important Arab leader, was now living in Berlin as the personal guest of Adolf Hitler.

Perhaps now, in the fifth month of the war, the British had finally decided to accept the help that the Jews in Palestine wanted to give. Perhaps they were using the *Hilda* as a sign to us—to the world—that the White Paper now would be torn up. Or forgotten. Perhaps that was why the *Hilda* had not been sent back to Rumania. Perhaps that was why the two British ships had brought her all the way to Palestine.

The next day another cable came from Palestine. We translated the code, and then sat, stunned. The British had ordered that the *Hilda* set sail at once for Paraguay, South America!

Paraguay!

The false passports we'd given our people listed Paraguay as their future home. We had to do this. We could hardly put down Palestine.

But our old leaking ship was barely fit to make it across the Mediterranean. To send her into the Atlantic Ocean was to send our passengers and crew to their death.

The next day Kadmon telephoned from Palestine.

"The latest news on the *Hilda?* Just listen!" he said.

First the captain had told the British that the ship was leaking badly. She needed repairs before she could put out to sea.

Overnight the Jews of Haifa had put posters up all over the city. The *Hilda* passengers must be allowed to land in Palestine!

The British did not answer.

Now the Jews of Palestine were planning a hunger strike.

Moshe and I looked at each other. Our 727 men and women were not all alone any longer.

On January 28 another cable came. The passengers on the *Hilda* had painted four words in large white letters on the side of the ship. WE WILL NOT LEAVE.

The next day the British met with a delegation of Jews in Haifa. The delegation was told they must get all the Jews to stop all talk of hunger strikes. At once.

A member of the Jewish delegation answered with a question. "Do you believe that there will be a single Jew who will not seek revenge if this ship is sent away?"

Our people were taken off the *Hilda*. The men were sent to a prison camp. The women were sent to an immigrant home. They were told that they would all be sent back to Europe.

But they were not sent back. Within six months they were all set free by the British.

The 727 men and women and the two babies, Hilda and Yehuda, became new citizens of Palestine.

WHAT HAPPENED THEN

Though the situation became ever more dangerous, Ruth Klüger refused to leave Rumania. She was trying desperately to organize another ship for the Kladovo people. But no ship could be found.

Then, in November 1940, the Iron Guard took over the country: "Rumanian Nazis." They drove out the king. They murdered sixty-four top Rumanian officials. Former criminals were now in power. Every day they passed new anti-Jewish laws.

On a snowy day in December a group of Iron Guardists hammered on the front door of the Schecter home. They had come to arrest Ruth. She escaped out the bathroom window, and made her way to Turkey.

While she was there a ship of illegals sank in the harbor off Istanbul. This was not a Mossad ship. It had been organized by a man who said he was in the business of saving Jews—if they paid enough for a passage. The ship he organized was called the Salvador, the Savior. It was an old sailing ship with a broken motor. A fierce storm broke out. The captain of the Salvador asked Turkish port authorities for permission to let the refugees land before the ship sank. Permission was refused. Two hundred thirty-one men, women, and children drowned that night.

Among those who drowned was Stefan Meta, the man Ruth was to marry.

Ruth fell ill. For weeks she was delirious. She kept calling for Stefan.

On January 23, 1941, she lay in bed, recovering. The radio was on. Soft music was interrupted by a long news report. Stiff with horror, Ruth listened to the report about the three-day wave of murders in Rumania. Murders of Jews.

They were murdered in horrible ways. Truckloads of professors, bankers, businessmen were taken to the woods outside of Bucharest. There they were forced to strip naked. Then they were machine-gunned. Their mutilated bodies were left in the snow to freeze.

Some who had fled to the synagogues to pray were locked in the buildings. Then the synagogues were set on fire.

Some were killed in the slaughterhouse. They were made to crawl naked up the ramp on their hands and knees, like animals. At the end of the ramp, heads were chopped off and thrown in a basket. Then the bodies were hung on meathooks and stamped KOSHER MEAT.

Among those murdered in this way was Moshe Orekhovsky.

Orekhovsky. The man in charge of legal certificates of entry into Palestine.

At all times Moshe had three legal certificates in his wall safe: for his wife, his small daughter, Rita, and for himself. He knew that the police were out to get him.

When the Iron Guard took over in Rumania, Ruth begged Orekhovsky to take his family and get out.

He refused to leave. "My work is here," he told her. Once, when she pleaded with him on the phone to leave—at once—he hung up on her. His daughter Rita later said it was the only time she ever saw her father hang up on anybody.

Moshe was not one of those who believed, it can't happen here. Ruth's brother David, her sister-in-law Sophie, their two children were now in a forced labor camp. Because they had believed it can't happen here. *Her brother Arthur, in Austria, was in a concentration camp. His wife was dead. Because they had believed* it can't happen here.

Moshe Orekhovsky was one of the few Jews in Europe who could have left at any time. He not only believed that it could happen here; he was certain that it would happen. And that was why he chose to stay. To help others get out.

He was murdered in the slaughterhouse at the age of forty.

Two weeks later his wife and daughter took the hour-long train trip to the port of Constanta, and left —legally—for Palestine.

Seven weeks after that, word came to Sima Spitzer that 250 legal certificates had been set aside so that the Kladovo children could be brought to Palestine.

On April 6, 1941, the children left. Many of them cried. They did not want to leave their parents. They did not want to go off alone to a strange country. But the parents knew that it could happen here. They insisted that their children go.

So the children left. They left in five groups of 50. When they had reached Greece they were put into a sealed train. Even though they all had legal certificates the Greek government would not permit the 250 Jewish children to pass through their country, unless they were locked up in the train.

They reached Palestine safely.

The same day that the children left, Hitler's armies smashed into Yugoslavia. They rounded up the Kladovo people. Some were made to dig deep trenches. Then they were told to stand at the edge. They were shot in the back. And they fell into the graves they had dug.

Others were given a chance to play a game. The Germans told them to scatter and run. Then the Germans ran after them, shooting them down, one by one, like rabbits in the field.

A few of the Kladovo women had married Yugoslavs. A few of the men had managed to escape. But all the rest of the Kladovo people—eleven hundred men and women—were murdered by the Germans on April 7, 1941.

Two months later Ruth received new orders.

It was no longer possible to operate in Europe.

Hitler had begun to put his "Final Solution" into operation. The Final Solution to the Jewish Question—that was the term.

Its meaning was—murder. Mass murder.

Kill all the Jews in all the countries Hitler had

conquered. And all the Jews in all the countries which had joined with him.

This included most of the nations of Europe.

Austria. Czechoslovakia. Poland. Norway. Denmark. Holland. Belgium. Luxembourg. France. Rumania. Greece. Yugoslavia. These countries had been taken over by Hitler.

Italy. Hungary. Bulgaria. These countries had joined with Germany. Spain too was Hitler's friend. And until June 1941, when Hitler invaded Russia, that country too had joined with Germany.

As each of these nations was taken over, doors slammed shut on the Jews. It was impossible to get out.

There was nothing the ten Mossad members could do now in Europe. But there were still Jews who could be reached; Jews who might soon be in terrible danger. Hundreds of thousands of Jews who lived in the Arab countries.

Ruth was asked to go to Egypt. There she would raise money and help organize a rescue operation to bring Jews from Egypt, Lebanon, Syria across the borders into Palestine.

Seven months later—in January 1942—a top secret conference was called by Hitler.

The Final Solution, said Hitler, was going too slowly. Jews were worked to death and starved to death in labor camps. Thousands were shot. Hundreds of thousands died of diseases which swept through the camps.

Jews who were not in camps had been herded into ghettos. There they were kept behind high walls, guarded by soldiers. There they starved, and died of disease.

But, complained Hitler, it was all too slow. Too slow.

After that conference the death camps with their gas chambers went into full operation. Nothing like them had ever been known in all of world history. They were huge factories with one product: Death.

In June 1944 American and British troops invaded Europe, from the West. Russian troops were pushing back Hitler's armies from the East. By August it was clear that Germany would lose the war. Orders went through from Hitler's headquarters: speed up the killing of Jews while there still is time.

Day and night trainloads of Jews were brought to the death camps. In Auschwitz, as many as 20,000 Jews were killed every day in the gas chambers. But the ovens could only burn up 12,000 dead bodies a day. So eight huge open pits were dug—each four by sixty yards wide. Here bodies were burned to cinders. Sometimes children were thrown alive into the blazing flames.

The war in Europe ended in May 1945.

In the four years from 1941 to 1945, two thirds of the Jews in Europe—some six million men, women, and children—lost their lives.

In 1944 Ruth Klüger was sent to Europe as the official representative of the Jews of Palestine. She was the first Jew from Palestine to enter the death camps a day or so after they were opened by the British and the American armies.

She started at once to organize more secret ships— like the Hilda.

After the war most of the Jewish survivors had no place to go. Their homes had been destroyed. They had no money. Many of the survivors had lost their entire family.

They did not want to go "back home." They had no home. Only ghastly memories.

They wanted to start a new life in a new land.

And hundreds of thousands wanted to return to the homeland they had never seen. The ancient Jewish homeland: Palestine.

Now that the war was over, surely the British who ruled in Palestine would tear up the White Paper. Surely they would let the survivors return to their ancient homeland.

Many Britons agreed that now—after the holocaust—the Jews should—indeed, must—have their own country: Palestine. But the British Foreign Minister, Ernest Bevin, said that the White Paper would remain in effect. It would remain in effect even though the number of legal certificates which had been promised would soon be used up. This meant that there would soon be no more legal immigration to Palestine permitted at all.

So the Mossad continued its work.

The secret ships continued to sail.

Many of the ships were caught by the British. Some of the illegals were sent back to Europe. There they lived in camps for people who had no home or homeland.

Some of the illegals were sent to the island of Cyprus. There the British kept them under armed guard in huge camps.

But some of the illegals got through.

It happened mainly on moonless nights. The Mossad organized fleets of small boats. Illegals were lowered from a ship to the little boats. They were rowed ashore, and landed on a deserted beach in Palestine.

There trucks and farmers' wagons were waiting to carry them off and hide them. And after a while they became Jewish citizens of Palestine; citizens with papers given to them by the Mossad.

On November 29, 1947, the United Nations voted that there should be a new Jewish nation in the ancient Jewish homeland: Palestine.

But would the Jews dare to declare themselves a new nation?

Seven Arab countries announced that they would go to war at once, if the Jews did declare their own state in Palestine. Most of the Arab nations were huge. The new Jewish nation would be tiny and skinny. The Arab nations had a total population of some fifty million. The new Jewish nation would have only some 650,000 Jews—including children.

King Ibn Saud of Saudi Arabia put it this way: "With fifty million Arabs, what does it matter if we lose ten million to kill all the Jews. The price is worth it."

Nor did the Jews have any arms. Their "air force," for example, was a few small Piper Cubs. Their "bombs" were grenades, mostly handmade.

Famous military experts came to Palestine to look over the situation. Some said it would take three days *for the Arabs to drive the Jews into the sea. Some said the Jews might hold out for ten days. All said that the new Jewish nation could never survive a war with seven Arab states.*

Nevertheless, on May 14, 1948, the Jews declared that their new nation had been born in part of the Biblical land of Palestine. They named their country Israel. And they opened their nation to any Jew from any land who wished to come.

Several hours after the state of Israel was officially born, the seven Arab countries declared war. Their armies invaded. And their fighters and bombers flew low over cities and farm settlements, dropping bombs.

The Israelis called this the War of Independence.

It took seven months. But Israel won.

Yet, *if it had not been for the thousands of Jews smuggled into Palestine between 1938 and 1948, Israel could not have won that war.* At the time the nation was born, one out of every three Israelis was an illegal. *Two hundred thousand Jews had been smuggled into the country, in the movement begun by nine men and the beautiful young redhead named Ruth. Their tiny group, the Mossad, had started the largest secret rescue movement of all time.*

The story of the secret ship, the Hilda, is therefore a symbol of all the other secret ships. And it was these ships and the men, women, and children they carried, which enabled Israel to survive.

The 727 men and women on the Hilda and the two infants born on the ship were also symbols. Symbols of all the illegals. Some of the Hilda passengers became famous in Israel. Among the people whose lives had been saved on the Hilda were well-known doctors, lawyers, chemists, musicians, artists, actresses, a dancer, an engineer, an architect.

But most of the men and women on the Hilda did not become famous. Yet, they like all the illegals, were indispensable.

They worked draining swamps to make new farm lands. They worked laying pipelines so that parts of the desert could be made to bloom. They worked in the schools, in the shops, in factories. They built new roads, new buildings, new farm communities, new towns.

Perhaps Yehuda is the best symbol of all the illegals. Yehuda—who was born on the Hilda.

He grew up in a kibbutz; a communal farm.

He was seventeen when he went to war for the first time; the '56 Sinai Campaign—his country's second war of survival. He was too young to be drafted. But he drove a milk truck to and from the front. His truck carried soldiers, many of whom did not even have uniforms. He thus took part in one of the most amazing wars in history. Within one hundred hours the Army of Israel slashed across the vast Sinai desert to the Suez Canal. They destroyed the bases from which Egyptian terrorists had been attacking Israel. They knocked out one third of the Egyptian Army, which had been mobilized on Israel's border, ready to attack. And they destroyed or captured vast amounts of arms and tanks which the Russians had given to the Egyptians.

After this "weekend war" Yehuda went back to his kibbutz. He finished school. He worked as a farmer. He married a sabra—a native-born Israeli.

They had three children.

When Yehuda was twenty-seven, he went to war again. Again he fought on the Egyptian front; this time as an army officer.

Egypt had massed 80,000 troops and nearly 1,000 tanks on Israel's border. Nasser, the Egyptian leader, announced, "The armies of Egypt, Jordan, Syria and Lebanon are stationed on the borders of Israel. . . . Behind them stand the armies of Iraq, Algeria, Kuwait, Sudan, and the whole of her Arab nation. . . . The hour of decision has arrived."

The President of Iraq summed it up simply. "The clear aim is to wipe Israel off the map."

This time the war took six days. Israel won. But she lost many soldiers.

Yehuda was badly wounded. He was sent to the hospital. He recovered. He went back home to the kibbutz; back to work.

When Yehuda was thirty-three, the Egyptians, Syrians, and Jordanians attacked Israel on Yom Kippur, the holiest day in the Jewish calendar. Once again he left the kibbutz and went to fight. Once again he was an officer in the army. Once again he was wounded. Once again he was sent to the hospital. Once again he recovered. And went back to work.

Yehuda—he was born on a ship of Jews heading toward the homeland.

He grew up in the new Jewish nation; in the ancient Jewish land.

He fought for his country's right to survive . . . was wounded . . . recovered . . . went back to work . . . fought again . . . was wounded . . . recovered . . . went back to work. . . .

He may be more than a symbol of those who came on the secret ships. He may be a symbol of Israel. Indeed, he may be a symbol of the Jewish people throughout the centuries.

Yehuda—the Hebrew word for Jew.